William Gaskill

D0492317

William Gaskill was born and brought up in Shipley, Yorkshire. His first London productions were as one of the associates of George Devine in the early days of the English Stage Company at the Royal Court Theatre. Writers whose plays he premiered include John Osborne, N.F. Simpson, Arnold Wesker, John Arden and Edward Bond. He was invited by Laurence Olivier to be an Associate Director in the founding of the National Theatre and in its first season directed a production of *The Recruiting Officer*, which brought a whole new approach to Restoration Comedy. A great advocate of the plays of Brecht, he directed many of the first British performances of Brecht's major plays. When George Devine retired in 1965 he asked Gaskill to take over the running of the Royal Court. Among the plays that he directed in his seven years as Artistic Director were all the early plays of Edward Bond, among them *Saved*. Though unlicensed for public performance by the Lord Chamberlain (at that time responsible for licensing all plays), the production of *Saved* went ahead with the result that Gaskill and the English Stage Company were successfully prosecuted. The outcry that followed was important in the campaign to change the law, and in 1968 a bill was passed removing the Lord Chamberlain's powers of censorship. When Gaskill left the Royal Court he joined with Max Stafford-Clark in forming the Joint Stock Theatre Group and together they directed its opening productions: *The Speakers*, *Fanshen* and *Yesterday's News*. During his entire career Gaskill has always combined teaching with directing. Most of his recent work has been at the Royal Academy of Dramatic Art. His productions there include adaptations of Raymond Carver short stories and a chapter of James Joyce's *Ulysses*, and the first British stage production of Beckett's *All That Fall*. William Gaskill died in 2016.

William Gaskill

Words into Action

Finding the Life of the Play

Foreword by Christopher Hampton

NICK HERN BOOKS
London
www.nickhernbooks.co.uk

A Nick Hern Book

Words into Action
first published in Great Britain in 2010
by Nick Hern Books Limited, The Glasshouse,
49A Goldhawk Road, London W12 8QP

Reprinted 2011, 2016

Cover design by Peter Bennett

Typeset by Nick Hern Books, London
Printed and bound in Great Britain by
Ashford Colour Press, Gosport, Hampshire

A CIP catalogue record for this book
is available from the British Library

ISBN 978 1 84842 100 4

MIX
Paper from
responsible sources
FSC
www.fsc.org   FSC® C011748

To the memory of George Devine
and Jocelyn Herbert

Contents

Foreword—Christopher Hampton   ix

Preface   xiii

Acknowledgements   xv

1. Trusting the Writer—the Royal Court   1

2. Basic Lessons—Brecht and Beckett   7

3. What is an Action?—Ibsen and Chekhov   15

4. Action and Inaction—*Hamlet*   21

5. Talking to the Audience   35

6. Stage Directions   41

7. Action for the Actor   55

8. Action and Intention   61

9. Movement and Stillness—the Noh Theatre   69

10. Sentences and Rhetoric—Wilde, Webster and Winston Churchill   75

11. Phrasing and Pauses—Congreve and Beckett   87

12. Masks and Action—Ben Jonson   99

13. Language as Subject Matter   107

14. Verse and Prose—*Hamlet* again   115

15. The Words of Puritans—Shaw and Bunyan   123

16. Action and Imagination—*Macbeth*   127

17. Stress, Metre and Pitch   133

18. Magic and Metaphor—*The Tempest* and *Henry VIII*   145

19. Words and Music   151

20. State of Play   157

    Index   163

Foreword—Christopher Hampton

I have more than one reason to be grateful to Bill Gaskill: as Artistic Director of the Royal Court Theatre he was responsible, in 1966, for scheduling my first play as a Sunday-night 'Production Without Décor'; then, in 1968, he devised for me the position of Resident Dramatist at the theatre, now, of course, a commonplace, but at that time, I believe, the first such post of its kind in this country. Characteristically, he told me I need not be deceived by the important-sounding lustre of the title, which he regarded merely as a useful negotiating ploy to secure a grant from the Arts Council; I would be expected to run the literary department and perform any and all other delegated tasks. This made the gift doubly valuable: instead of sitting in my quarters writing plays (the fate, I imagine, of subsequent and current Resident Dramatists) I became thoroughly immersed in the day-to-day life of the theatre—then at one of its creative zeniths as one of the leading theatres in Europe—for two crowded years, in which I learned considerably more about the practicalities of my profession than I could possibly have picked up in any other way.

So much for my personal feelings of gratitude: but there are other, broader reasons for many contemporary playwrights to offer their thanks to a Royal Court ethos, of which Bill was one of the founders and which the essays in this book go a long way towards defining. 'When I start preparing a production,' he says, 'I always work from the text outwards'—and the book's starting point is a chapter called 'Trusting the Writer'. Those of us who have worked on the continent—in Germany, Austria, Switzerland or France—will be vividly aware just how alien a concept this is in other European countries, where directors are utterly baffled by the notion of presenting a play to their critics and public as written. As it happens, Bill begins his consideration of writers with Beckett (who lived in Paris and wrote the majority of his plays initially in French) and Brecht: but these writers above all—Beckett with his strict notations and Brecht with his own generously funded Ensemble—knew how to maintain an iron control over their work. For those of us less confident and in less powerful positions, the determination of Bill and his cohorts at the Royal Court to search out the essence of our plays and respect it was absolutely invaluable. My second play, *Total Eclipse*, about the poets Arthur Rimbaud and Paul Verlaine, started rehearsal when I arrived to work at the theatre in 1968; Bill liked it and was encouraging. He listened sympathetically to the reservations the director, Robert Kidd, and I both felt about the play, then said that, certainly, there were things wrong with it, but that I was very young and would learn most if the play, with all its imperfections, appeared in front of an audience as I had first imagined it. He was, of course, unquestionably right, though it's almost inconceivable that a writer would be given that kind of leeway today. It's my firm conviction that one of the essential preconditions for a healthy theatre is this kind of moral support and robust nurture of playwrights; it exists in very few parts of the world, but its centrality as a feature of Bill's regime in Sloane Square was of incalculable benefit to all the writers who passed through the doors of the Royal Court Theatre.

One of the great beauties of the theatre is its ephemerality. Films (doubly so with the advent of the DVD), books and records are all permanent, filable objects; but the theatre is written on the wind. Obviously, a play exists on paper, but its only real being is in the present tense and subsequently in the memories of however many thousand people may have chosen to experience it. I had the privilege, when I was at the Royal Court, of making a version, for Anthony Page, of *Uncle Vanya*, with Paul Scofield, Colin Blakely and Anna Calder-Marshall. It ran for only a few weeks forty years ago, but I can still remember it in considerable detail and hear, in my inner ear, the particular woebegone and embittered cadences, the eccentric swoop and plunge of Scofield's voice. Bill has always been as strong a champion of actors as he is of writers, and his book explores in fascinating detail his experience with actors like Maggie Smith and Alec Guinness and his memories of Gielgud, Olivier and Edith Evans. It's precisely the evanescence of the theatre which makes statements of first principles so essential, especially when expressed with Bill's exemplary lucidity. Every generation in the theatre has in some sense to start from scratch, lessons learned are seldom retained, and it's this fragile ecology which accounts for the numerous black holes in theatrical history, the long, arid stretches when no one can quite remember how to practise this most rigorous and demanding of arts.

Let me try to illustrate my point with a couple of specific examples: two of Bill's productions I saw at the turn of the seventies, Edward Bond's *Saved* and George Farquhar's *The Beaux' Stratagem*. Again, one is reliant on the images provided by memory, but in the one case, a kind of spare, poetic naturalism supported by John Gunter's pared-to-the-essentials, resonant sets, and in the other case, a supple, good-humoured, recognisably truthful narrative, lightened by René Allio's graceful, fluid, dancing pieces of décor and as far as possible removed from the usual grating artificiality of Restoration Comedy, each provided, in their very different ways, an object-lesson in how to discover the style which most perfectly complemented the substance of each of these plays. These are lessons, as I say, which can be easily, swiftly and lavishly forgotten: and the patient detail in these essays, the attention to stress and pause, lighting and design, timing and music, as applied to numerous specific plays and writers, remind us how important but how rarely pursued is the quest to present a play in a way which teases out, honours and clarifies the author's intentions, even those which he or she may not have been conscious of harbouring in the first place. The distance between good and bad theatre is far shorter than the distance that separates the good from the unforgettable; it is this latter terrain that Bill Gaskill patrols, contemplates and elucidates, as a true keeper of the flame.

Preface

These essays are about the way drama works in the theatre; drama in the sense that a play is about—and has always been about—people talking to each other in recognisable situations. It is about words and how they move an action forward, how words are actions, how words convey a physical staging not just through stage directions, and how the relation of actions to words makes for the tension of drama. It is about the form and diction of the language as indications to the actor, not just of his character, but of the shifts and changes in the meaning of the play as a whole. Some of it is a statement of the obvious, but necessary because we have lost touch with essentials. Some of it is made up of practical tips about speaking. Some of it is pleasure at memories of performances and some of it is wonder at the skill of the writer, particularly Shakespeare.

William Gaskill

Acknowledgements

The author and publisher gratefully acknowledge permission to quote from *Poetry and Drama* by T.S. Eliot, *Endgame*, *Play* and *Waiting for Godot* by Samuel Beckett, *No Man's Land* by Harold Pinter, and *A Resounding Tinkle* by N.F. Simpson, all published by Faber and Faber Ltd; *A Guide to English Literature* by F.W. Bateson, published by Pearson Education Ltd; *Early Morning* and *Saved* by Edward Bond, both published by Methuen Drama, an imprint of A&C Black Publishers Ltd; *Exposed by the Mask* © Peter Hall (2000), published by Oberon Books Ltd; *Ulysses* by James Joyce, published by Penguin Books Ltd; John Berger's translations of Brecht, published by Scorpion Press; an extract from the *Saturday Review* (January 1897) by George Bernard Shaw, by kind permission of The Society of Authors on behalf of Shaw's estate; and Sir John Gielgud's letter to Richard Bebb (30 January 1976) from *Gielgud's Letters: John Gielgud in His Own Words*, edited by Richard Mangan, published by Weidenfeld & Nicolson Ltd, by kind permission of the trustees of the Sir John Gielgud Charitable Trust.

1
Trusting the Writer—the Royal Court

I was lucky to start my career at the Royal Court Theatre a year after it had become, in 1956, the home of the English Stage Company under the leadership of George Devine. It had been founded on a very simple basis. There was a need for new writing, for change in the theatre. The only way to find writers was to have a theatre that would put on new plays. What happened is a story staled by repetition: the arrival of *Look Back in Anger* and its almost immediate reception as a breakthrough in dramatic writing. It's all a long time ago. Those reading or seeing Osborne's play for the first time today may be puzzled as to why we felt so excited. But we did. It was immediately of our own time; speaking to us and for us. I remember my first reaction to reading it was not that it was controversial or political and certainly not avant-garde, but that it restored language to a robust rhetorical life. And it was only the beginning.

There was a succession of young writers—Ann Jellicoe, John Arden, Arnold Wesker—all in some way experimenting with language or dramatic form or staging. I discovered the excitement of working with a living writer for the first time. I had already done some time in weekly repertory companies as well as directing amateur productions at university, and I thought I knew what it was all about. My dream of a career was having more rehearsal time, of an ensemble developing new styles based on exploring what would now be called physical theatre. 'A writer's theatre'

1

seemed a necessary idea, but I didn't see it as basically altering my approach to directing. But I wanted to be in on this venture and was prepared to direct anything that was offered to me. My chance was one of the try-out Sunday-night productions.

N.F. Simpson, whose play *A Resounding Tinkle* was my first production at the Royal Court in 1957, was completely new to the theatre but his exploration of language and comic timing was wholly original. I didn't really understand the play. It had no story and progressed—if it could be called that—by a series of disconnected sequences, loosely held together by a middle-class couple debating how to name an elephant that had been delivered in their back garden, intercut with two comedians searching for the essence of comedy. It sounds rather precious but it has a gravitas and polish in the dialogue that sets it apart. It was only two years after the first British production of *Godot* and some years before *Monty Python*, on which it could be claimed to have some influence. Simpson, who knew little of stagecraft and avoided narrative more completely than Laurence Sterne, had a great deal to teach me. He probably only wrote the play because of a playwriting competition sponsored by the *Observer* and chaired by its drama critic, Kenneth Tynan, but he had a very clear idea of what would make the dialogue work when spoken, even though he didn't know where the actors would be on stage. In particular his awareness of time, of the relation of the pause to comic effect, was new to me. The response of the audience to the one performance of the play on a Sunday night proved he was right.

Working on a new play with a writer changed my whole approach to directing. The writer's exploration of form and of the nature of theatre experience meant I had to work more closely to the text than I had realised. There were times when I would know more than the writer but also many times when I had to be prepared to go down new roads with him or her. When I came to direct classics I already had experience of several living writers, and I tried to read the old writers as if I were in as close and direct contact with them as I was with the new. Sometimes I try to break away from this relationship but I have always returned to words as the starting point.

Devine was a protégé of the French director Michel Saint-Denis, a nephew and pupil of Jacques Copeau, and was very influenced by his attempts to recover the acting styles of the past—particularly the *Commedia dell'Arte*—and his insistence on the importance of building an ensemble of actors, directors, designers, technicians and writers. The first season at the Royal Court was built round a resident company, with staff designers and technicians. The productions were all by Devine or his associate Tony Richardson. Richardson had never been really interested in the Saint-Denis approach. He thought it dragged the theatre back into an arty past. The success of his production of *Look Back in Anger* in the first season validated his attitude. The ensemble was soon disbanded, though there were sporadic attempts to revive it. The writers had become the prime mover in the work. The discovery of style would be initiated by them. There were important continuities of design, mainly through the work of Jocelyn Herbert, and of directing, through the staff directors, who became linked to the work of particular writers: myself with Simpson and later Edward Bond, John Dexter with Arnold Wesker, and later Lindsay Anderson with David Storey, but the writer came first. It has been said by David Hare and Peter Gill, amongst others, that the Court was really a director's theatre and not a writer's theatre at all. It is true that Tony Richardson would ruthlessly cut Osborne's plays, Wesker's plays could not have been realised without the brilliant stagecraft of John Dexter, and David Storey owes a great deal to the poetic realism of

Lindsay Anderson's productions. On the other hand, George Devine always did what Beckett told him and so did I with Edward Bond. But for all of us the starting point was the writer's words.

As the Royal Court was starting in Sloane Square, Joan Littlewood and her Theatre Workshop were already at work in Stratford, East 15. Littlewood's idea of theatre was quite different. She too believed in the totality of the theatre experience in which writer, director, actors and designers were part of the same creative process, but the start of the work was in the theatricality of the actors' improvisation. No one, except perhaps she herself, was going to dominate. Certainly not the writer. She had a dedicated group of young actors—a true collective—on a share of the box office, often with barely enough to live on, who knew they would be cast in every play, however unsuited to the part. Instead of a play being written and then handed over to the interpreters, the writer was there in rehearsal, ready to rewrite at a moment's notice. It's true that writers were present at rehearsal in Sloane Square, but only to safeguard the sanctity of their text.

Littlewood's theatre used music, movement and, above all, improvisation to create the final experience. And it didn't stop there. Joan would go to every performance, give notes and make changes all through the run of the play. I once told her how moved I was by the end of *A Taste of Honey* and she promptly changed it. But it would be wrong to think of Theatre Workshop as 'Director's Theatre', as we would now use the phrase to describe the work of egomaniacs who impose their concepts on a play and any actors they happen to be working with. Joan's work was essentially that of a group making theatre together. The group would not have existed without her powerful personality and vison but it was still a group with a shared political viewpoint and with a social purpose.

I admired Joan but I was on the other side. I believed in the exactness of writing, the importance of the choice of words. Coleridge thought poetry was 'best words in the best order'. How would he have defined drama? 'Best actions in the best order', perhaps. Words too are actions and the sequence of words and actions and their interplay is the basis of dramatic writing.

2
Basic Lessons—Beckett and Brecht

As the Royal Court was starting its first season in 1956, Brecht's company the Berliner Ensemble was preparing to come to London. Brecht died before they left Berlin but the last thing he wrote was a note to his actors telling them that the British public thought that everything German was heavy, boring and slow and that, therefore, the actors had to play quickly and lightly.

Everyone on the intellectual left was keyed up for their arrival and at the opening night at the Palace Theatre there was animated discussion with John Berger, Christopher Logue, Lindsay Anderson and the rest about whether it was a completely new theatre experience, as we had been led to expect from Ken Tynan. The opening production was *The Caucasian Chalk Circle*. The simplicity but richness of the settings, the sense of actors moving in space, the cool unatmospheric lighting were all wonderful but it was the playing that most impressed us. Grusha, the simple peasant girl who saves the Governor's baby in the middle of a revolution and is allowed to keep him at the end, was played by Angelika Hurwicz, a homely dumpling of a girl who walked on the stage as if it were her native soil. She epitomised the open playing that Brecht wanted; realistically observed and with a sense of 'Look at this character, see what she does, see where she has to make decisions, judge whether they are the right ones.' Psychology and empathy were out, no searching of motivations or 'emotion memory', only an awareness of the character in society. That was the theory, and the playing of Hurwicz and the rest proved that it worked. When we saw *Mother Courage* a few nights later there was no doubt. This was a new theatre.

Courage, who pulls her wagon in the wake of the Thirty Years War and in the process loses her three children, was played by Brecht's widow Helene Weigel. Weigel was a tiny woman with skin stretched tightly over her cheekbones like a Japanese mask. She had hardly acted since leaving Germany in the 1930s until her return in 1949. As Courage, she was unparalleled. In one scene her second son, Swiss Cheese, has been caught and is about to be shot. Courage bargains through an intermediary, the whore Yvette, for her son's life. The final price is the wagon and all its contents, her livelihood. She hesitates and Yvette goes running off. Courage says, 'I have bargained too long,' and there is the sound of the firing squad offstage as Swiss Cheese is shot. When she heard the shot, Weigel arched her back, lifted her head and opened her mouth in a soundless cry. An unforgettable image. The scene that follows was remarkable. The son's body is brought onto the stage and we know it is essential that Courage must appear to have no connection with him. The soldiers ask her to look at the body. The body is on a stretcher downstage-right and Courage is sitting on a stool at the extreme left. Weigel gets up with her face fixed in a terrible rictus, supposed to be a smile, and crosses the great empty stage very, very slowly. She keeps the smile as she looks down at the body of her son and shakes her head, denying that she recognises him, but as she turns from the soldiers all the muscles of her face drop. Nothing could have been more technically controlled or more wonderful.

Brecht's actors were intensely serious in their detachment from their characters and in the focus on their actions. At no point were they concerned with identifying with the inner life of the people they played, but they cared about the decisions they took in their lives. At the same time their playing was as Brecht would have wished: light, almost casual, never portentous or aggressive.

The whole of Brecht's philosophy of theatre is contained in a series of wonderful poems. In one he describes how Weigel chose her props:

> According to age
> Uses
> And beauty
> By knowing eyes and her
> Net making, bread baking
> Soup cooking hands
> At home with reality
>
> (John Berger's translation)

In a story called *The Old Hat*, Brecht tells how he watched the actor playing Filch in *The Threepenny Opera* choose a hat for his part. He selects a possible two but is satisfied with neither of them. He considers them carefully.

> Had Filch's hat once been good or at least better than the other? How could it be exactly right? Did Filch take care of it when he took it off, if he was in a position to take care of it? Or was it a hat that he definitely didn't wear in his prosperous days?

In the end the actor makes a choice but is not happy.

> At the next rehearsal he showed me an old toothbrush sticking out of his jacket pocket, which demonstrated that Filch, even underneath the arches, still maintained the properties of civilised life. The toothbrush showed me that he was not at all satisfied with the best hat he could find. This, I thought happily, is an actor of the scientific age.

The impact of the Ensemble was immediate. This was what theatre should be. The simple but beautiful staging, the realistic acting, the clear lighting. All these could be copied but we could not copy the conditions that had produced the work or the unifying purpose of the people involved in it. Brecht had returned to Berlin with a sackful of plays written in his exile, with actors he had worked with in the 1920s and '30s like Weigel and Ernst Busch, and with his original designer Caspar Neher. He was the main writer and also the director of the company who had evolved his approach to the theatre and was ready to put it into practice. And the company was held together by a shared political attitude.

We tried to absorb some of Brecht's approach to theatre in our work in the early years at the Royal Court, but his theatre style came from his writing. Our writers were all writing in different styles and exploring new theatre forms. Osborne used the device of the music hall to open up *The Entertainer*, but he is essentially an enclosed writer and his canvas is the small family unit, however fractured. The anarchic satire of Simpson was also centred on the family. Wesker's plays were political but soft-centred. Only John Arden easily fitted into an idea of 'Epic Theatre' with his songs and broad social picture, but even he was too much of a free spirit to conform to a rigid political programme. The most lasting influence of the Ensemble was on design and staging. Jocelyn Herbert, the designer, more than anyone else absorbed the Brechtian idea of essential elements on an otherwise bare stage and blended it with a kind of English romanticism so that it became the Royal Court house-style, which could include the naturalism of Wesker's trilogy and Storey's plays of workers and rugby players, as well as the larger canvas of Arden. Her designs for Brecht's *Baal* and *Saint Joan of the Stockyards* were poetic but never sentimental. She also became the chosen designer for the plays of Samuel Beckett.

While we younger directors were trying to balance the experience of the undoubted rightness of Brecht's work with the kind of plays that were being written, Beckett had arrived on the scene. *Waiting for Godot* was first directed in English by Peter Hall at the Arts Theatre in 1955, but in 1957

George Devine managed to arrange that the world premiere of the French production of *Fin de partie* should take place at the Royal Court. A production of the English translation, *Endgame*, was scheduled for the following year and, after a ridiculous spat with the censor, went ahead. Devine was directing and also playing Hamm, the amazing Jackie Mac-Gowran was playing Clov. Beckett came over to watch rehearsals. Devine was very nervous and stumbled all over the place but very gently Beckett calmed him down, and to all intents and purposes took over the production. Beckett had not yet fully acquired the taste for directing his own plays, but he was more dominant in the rehearsals of *Happy Days* in 1962. We would watch him from the upper circle and though we had a great respect for him we were not in awe and certainly had no sense of the cult figure he subsequently became. In those early days 'avant-garde' was a dirty word in Sloane Square. We were for a positive Socialist theatre made by British writers and, for us younger directors, Beckett was classed with Ionesco as the Paris-based 'High Art' we were trying to get away from. They even wrote in French. Our tastes were probably more catholic than that, but battle lines had been drawn. Ken Tynan had a public debate with Ionesco, and one of his last notices for the *Observer*, before becoming Literary Manager of the National Theatre, was a damning notice of *Krapp's Last Tape*, entitled 'Slamm's Last Knock'.

In the first season at the National Theatre I was directing a production of Sophocles' *Philoctetes* which was to share a double bill with the British premiere of Beckett's *Play*, directed by Devine. *Play* is about a man, his wife and his mistress, all presumably dead, each buried up to the neck in an urn. They are forced by a probing light to recount endlessly the story of their past relationship, as if they were in some Dantesque version of Hell. At the end of the piece they start all over again. The actors—Robert Stephens, Billie Whitelaw and Rosemary Harris—were directed to speak the lines in a monotone at a breakneck pace. This was what Beckett wanted. The first run was watched by Olivier, Tynan and myself. Olivier and Tynan were horrified by the pace; they couldn't grasp the sense as the words flew by and they tried to persuade Beckett and Devine to slow it down. I agreed with them. Devine stood firmly by his writer and nothing was changed. He was proved right in performance when the relentless pace became an experience in itself. In fact it was so much more exciting than *Philoctetes* that their position in the double bill was reversed and the Sophocles became the curtain-raiser to the Beckett. (I have a feeling that when you know what the characters are saying it is even more exciting but the decision on the speed was the right one.)

Beckett never theorised about what theatre should be or what it was for. He knew how his plays should be done and that was enough. He wasn't really interested in their effect on an audience and never watched his plays once they had opened. But if we try and formulate the aesthetic principles of his theatre practice it might not end up a million miles from Bertolt Brecht:

> Only have on the stage what is essential to the action.
> Don't move the actors unless it means something.
> Every property and every costume has meaning.

There is one area in which they would have differed. Brecht believed in a clear, diffused light:

> Electrician
> Give us light on our stage.
> How can we disclose
> We playwright and actors
> Images to the world in semi-darkness?
> The sleepy darkness sends to sleep
>
> (John Berger's translation)

Beckett's world—at least after *Godot*—is a world of darkness, in his later plays a darkness only stabbed by spotlights. It's an enclosed world of the poet's imagination, and a metaphor, if not for our own time, of the future that will come. Brecht's world is for political examination with a hope of positive change.

We theatre workers adopted the aesthetics of Brecht but not for the same political ends. In my production of *Macbeth* at the Royal Court in 1966, I flooded the stage with bright white light. My idea was that the atmosphere was all in the text and needed no artificial help, that the essential meaning of the play would be clear: that there is a darkness of the mind as well of the sky. It was a bold idea but it demanded too much of an audience and the actors. Shakespeare may have written the play for the open-air Globe, but even in the open air the sun does not shine all the time. Soon after writing the play his company began using a second, indoor theatre at Blackfriars, where they would have played *Macbeth* lit by candles. They probably loved hiding in the darkness. On a proscenium stage you cannot create the equivalent of outdoor lighting. Even at the Berliner Ensemble, the full blast of open white light was only used in key moments. When I did *Macbeth* many years later at RADA in a promenade production, it was more like Beckett. The lighting was dynamic rather than atmospheric, light coming out of darkness to lead the audience round the space. It worked much better.

It is interesting that it is Beckett, writing puzzling plays set in unspecific locations, in an enclosed world, who has been accepted as creating the stage metaphors for our own time; Brecht, who so specifically wrote narratives which would be meaningful for our political situation, now fails to connect, at least in this country.

Both writers were poets, though Beckett is more often thought of as a novelist. People who know German think Brecht was a better poet than playwright. I am not qualified to say. But it is Beckett who is the more original poet of theatre.

3
What is an Action?—Ibsen and Chekhov

What is an action? Something performed, completed, done, but also a movement forward. In the theatre it can mean many things. For Aristotle it meant the succession of events, in his theory the most important element of theatre. It can mean the physical things that are done by the actor on the stage which we used to call 'business'. In a method used by Max Stafford-Clark and other directors it is an analysis of what an actor is doing by saying each line of the text. I want to look at all of these and particularly how each speech moves the action of the play forward and what that means to the actor.

The overall action, the movement of a play, is a primary experience of an audience. Watching Anthony Page's production of *Rosmersholm* at the Almeida Theatre (2008) I found myself gripped like a child by the development of the plot. I know the play well but I was as excited by what would happen next as when I first heard it on the radio as a boy. There is no spare fat in the writing. Everything moves the action forward, and we can feel it move. I was riveted by Rebecca West's final confession that she is responsible for the first wife's suicide, which leads to the denouement. The ending has been signalled from the very first pages of the play. In the opening scene, Rebecca is crocheting a white shawl. She and the housekeeper watch through the window to see whether Rosmer will cross the bridge over the mill race, where his wife committed suicide. At the end the housekeeper watches as Rebecca, now wearing the white shawl, and Rosmer throw themselves off the footbridge. The doom of the House of Rosmer is fulfilled. But is it not all just too pat? Is there no more positive outcome for the characters' dilemma? Then I thought of the ending of *Little Eyolf*, when Allmers and Rita try to put the past behind them and take up social work, which doesn't feel any more satisfactory, either morally or theatrically. All plays have to get somewhere and our sense of the rightness of the ending will change over the years. Today the idea that a moral dilemma can be stated in terms of the lives of individuals, let alone be resolved, is unacceptable. The double suicide in *Rosmersholm* or the avalanche on the mountain in *When We Dead Awaken* seem to us a cop-out, just as we can no longer accept the arrival of Fortinbras to take over Denmark or Malcolm's victory in Scotland as satisfactory conclusions to the tragedies that precede them. We prefer the desolate ending of *King Lear*, or the cynical ending of *Troilus and Cressida*, when Pandarus bequeaths us his diseases.

The most radical change in the nature of concluding a play came with Chekhov. He brought the quality of short-story writing to the theatre, and, though he used some of the elements of melodrama, he rooted his plays firmly in the day-to-day existence of people. It is true that at the end of his first major play, *The Seagull*, Konstantin commits suicide but it happens almost casually. He has already failed to kill himself earlier in the play, and when he does—offstage—it is not felt to be an inevitable ending. Nor does his story, his action, occupy the entire centre of the play. It is shared with that of Nina, the girl who has suffered and learned to endure. Together with Arkadina and Trigorin they present four variations on the theme of artistic creativity. Indeed each character seems central to the action while they are in focus. None of them has heroic status: their suffering, their struggles are of the same kind as ours watching. This lack of heroism is a significant shift in drama. Chekhov called his plays comedies because there was no alternative. He looks at the strivings and aspirations of human beings and shows how hopeless they are. Whether you find them funny or not is up to you, but they are certainly not tragic. Ibsen tried desperately to cut his characters down to size by exposing their weaknesses, but Solness and Borkman, however flawed, still retain heroic and tragic stature.

Chekhov also changed the nature of action. Instead of the inexorable progression of events he made an action that feels like a part of a continuous existence. Instead of the dramatic full stop of the final curtain you have life going on. In *The Cherry Orchard*, Firs is left to die in the empty house and we hear the breaking string we heard earlier, but the orchard is being chopped down for a purpose, and there will be a new, if different, life ahead. It's better than the mill race. In Ibsen the narrative is manipulated to make a statement; in Chekhov we have the feeling of life as it is. But in any play we still seek something akin to what Aristotle called action, a succession of events during the time we have been in the theatre, which we think must be meaningful, even if negative.

Even in the most experimental play you know when it's over. Plays with little obvious narrative are held together by some sense of movement. In pre-twentieth-century plays action moved forwards through time in a straight line. Beckett takes us through cycles. We think we are moving forward but find ourselves back at the beginning. In *Waiting for Godot* the second act finishes exactly like the first, with the two tramps motionless. We imagine another day in which they may wait again without success, but having watched them wait twice we have seen enough to get the writer's point. Or think we have. In *Play* the protagonists tell and retell their stories through all eternity. Mother Courage in Brecht's play goes through the history of the Thirty Years War, losing her children, but at the end is still pulling her wagon against the revolving stage and getting nowhere. The years have moved on but the action is the same.

When I first worked in a weekly repertory company, actors spent much of the rehearsal time adding 'business', small actions undescribed in the text, to give credibility or reality to their character—or just to keep their hands busy. The most usual was lighting a cigarette. Every piece of furniture on the set had an ashtray with a little water in it to make sure the cigarette went out after it had been put down. As we became more serious about our work we started to see that every physical action done on the stage must mean something and that even the smallest of actions like pouring a cup of tea will be significant if it is focused on or played more slowly. You can ritualise anything by the way that you do it. A simple action like serving bread and wine becomes ritualised in the Eucharist. *Hoc est corpus...* the body and blood of Christ. With the elevation of the Host in church it is no longer important to stress the ritual manner because the audience/congregation has agreed to accept its symbolic meaning, it can be done automatically. In the theatre the actor and director have to create the ritualisation, to show the physical action as expressive of something more. Peter Gill in his productions of D.H. Lawrence's plays understood that the daily washing of a miner's back is sacramental. In the last scene of *The Widowing of Mrs Holroyd*, the washing of the dead miner is a repeat of the ritual of the living man, but it is also the preparation of the corpse for burial.

The finished narrative is like the completed sentence. Both are linear. Ritual is not. Ritual, like music, uses repetition. You keep returning to the same theme in variation. In theatre there is a pull between ritual and action: the action that moves you forward and the ritual that opens sideways to show the universal significance of what is being done. Very few plays have a narrative drive with no expansion or digression. *Rosmersholm* is one of them, but compare it to a Greek tragedy, which, in many ways, it resembles. In the Greek play the choruses interrupt the narrative and give it a larger meaning. The interruption changes our experience of the play. This is mirrored in the form of the Greek stage in which the action is played out by actors on the raised platform at the back while the chorus sings and dances in the huge *orchestra* in the middle of the audience, creating the ritual.

Action also differs from old-fashioned storytelling. Stories that we are told as children fascinate us by what happens, however strange. The stories may mean something but we don't know what. The narrative is everything. A play is not quite like that. The basic story of *Oedipus* is essentially the same in all versions, but it is the way it is told by Sophocles, the precise succession of events which give the play its identity. Even *Hamlet* was based on an earlier play that the original audience knew. It is the different stress or the variation of the details of the story which makes us feel that this particular version has something to say, that the story has a meaning which can relate to our own lives.

Francis Fergusson in his book *The Idea of a Theater* gives examples of the action of the whole play expressed in one sentence. The action of *Oedipus* is the discovery of the murderer of Laius, the action of *The Cherry Orchard* is the sale of the cherry orchard, and so on. But this still begs the question, 'What does the play mean?' The realisation by Oedipus of who the murderer of Laius is and the action he takes because of his discovery bring the play to its final statement. The relentless search instigated by the king at the beginning of the play, in order to lift the plague from the city, is as clearly defined as any detective story. But the consequences of his discovery are necessary to complete the dramatic ritual.

4
Action and Inaction—*Hamlet*

What is the action of *Hamlet*? The avenging of the murder of Hamlet's father? It is not an adequate description of our experience of the play. If Hamlet did not kill Claudius at the end we should feel cheated, but we know it is not what the play is about. The energy of the play is not driven by a character's need for revenge, as it is in *The Revenger's Tragedy*. In the very first speech of the Middleton/Tourneur play, Vindice has a soliloquy in which he tells us what he is going to do and why. In the rest of the play he does it. In Hamlet's first soliloquy he tells us he is unhappy because his mother has married his father's brother. He has no idea what to do and decides to keep quiet. Our first insight into his mind— which is so inconclusive—colours our feeling about not only the character but about the actions or lack of actions which are to follow. In a modern play the material of Hamlet's soliloquy might be enough reason for him to kill Claudius. In 1600 the audience had to have the trappings of the 'revenge play' to justify it.

Hamlet is a play about—among a thousand other things— play-acting. Two of its great scenes are about the theatre: the arrival of the Players, and the play scene itself. Hamlet claims he is not playing a part by wearing mourning:

> These indeed seem,
> For they are actions that a man might play
>
> (*Hamlet* 1.2)

but very soon he is playing the part of a madman. He plays at being an actor when he speaks the 'rugged Pyrrhus' speech in front of the professional actors, he is a director in the 'advice to the Players', and he is an audience in the play scene. If he had been cast as the King he might have been very good.

> For he was likely, had he been put on,
> To have proved most royally.

> (*Hamlet* 5.2)

There is a clear comparison between the Player's convincing imitation of emotion—'tears in's eyes, distraction in's aspect'—and Hamlet's lack of demonstrated feeling. The answer to poor play-acting is to proceed to action itself, to the doing not the pretending. In the conflict of these two ideas, the inactive feeling and the unfelt doing, is the paradox of the character and the meaning of the play.

In key moments where the action becomes physical and the narrative is moved forward by violence, like the sudden killing of Polonius, we feel the actions of the protagonist are somehow unrelated to the gravitas of a ritual fulfilment. Hamlet is acting on an almost irresponsible impulse. When he finally comes to kill Claudius he does it on the spur of the moment, because he has discovered the treachery of the poisoned rapier rather than after five acts of inexorable fate fulfilling the demands of his father. The required action of the play—the death of Claudius—is Hamlet's responsibility, which he has avoided. It's like a bus rushing along with Hamlet standing on the pavement deciding whether to jump on or not and then almost missing the step as he leaps. Suddenly he's there and the bus is arriving at its destination but he's not driving.

Most critics agree that *Hamlet* stands midpoint in Shakespeare's development, not quite a tragedy in the sense of the later, more centred tragedies, yet radical in its exploration of the relation of character to action. Before *Hamlet* the

men of action know what they want and where they are
going—Richard III and Henry V (the great parts of Laurence Olivier, the actor par excellence of ruthless,
undebated action). The action and the character are one.
The opening soliloquy of *Richard III* sets in motion the play.
'This is what I'm going to do. Now watch me do it.' After
Hamlet there are always doubts. 'This is what I feel and is
this what I should do?' For the first time the inner life of
the character becomes important, not just as part of the
plot but as something to be explored in its own right. The
play uses language as it had never been used before, leaping
from verse to prose and back again, with the utmost variety
of style, to cope with the new demands. Hamlet asks the
question, 'What am I going to do? What must I do so as not
to lose the name of action?' He would like to become water:

> O, that this too, too solid flesh would melt,
> Thaw and resolve itself into a dew…

—but he can't.

The basic metaphor of action as opposed to inaction is
most vividly expressed in the Player's speech from the play
about the fall of Troy. He is describing Pyrrhus about to kill
Priam:

> For lo, his sword,
> Which was declining on the milky head
> Of reverend Priam, seemed i'the air to stick.
> So as a painted tyrant Pyrrhus stood
> And like a neutral to his will and matter
> Did nothing.
>
> *(Hamlet* 2.2)

Three scenes later Hamlet is in exactly the same situation.
He discovers Claudius praying, raises his sword to kill him,
and pauses. For Pyrrhus this is only a pause before the
action is carried through. Hamlet does nothing. He justifies
his inaction to us—or to himself—and goes off to see his
mother, which the Freudians would tell us is what it's all

about. One action has been rejected in favour of another. The delay creates new catastrophes. The killing of Polonius, about which he has no hesitation and no remorse, produces the madness of Ophelia; and the two actions together bring back Laertes from Paris for revenge. Laertes' return is used by Claudius for his own ends. The delay has caused the catastrophe. Sometimes it feels as if it is Shakespeare delaying, not his protagonist, as if he doesn't want to resolve the action or feels dissatisfied with what form it will take if he does. Certainly no play has such outrageous digressions: the discussion of the success of the boys' companies—the 'little eyases'—or the fencing skill of Monsieur Lamord being among the worst. They are impossible to justify, either as narrative or thematically, by even the most sophistical apologist. These are not character delays: they are the author's, for whatever reason.

The play is a series of variations on action and inaction and their interplay. Can inaction be as interesting as action? Three centuries later Beckett answers the question with an assured 'Yes'. Both acts of *Waiting for Godot* end in the same way:

> VLADIMIR. Well, shall we go?
> ESTRAGON. Yes, let's go.
> *They do not move.*

They feel the need for action but do nothing. Yet the circular, aimless conversation, the futile, unfulfilled action, are the meaning of the play. The digressive rhythm of *Hamlet* (or Shakespeare's obsession with it) is also central to our experience. The not going is as important as the going; the not being as being.

Mark Antony in *Julius Caesar* knows what he is doing. In his speech over the dead body of Caesar he incites the mob to turn against the conspirators. His words create the action. In the brilliant short scene that follows we see the mob in mindless violence beating up a totally innocent man. But in a sense Antony's speech is an action too; the persuading of the mob is as much an action as the physical actions he sets in motion. We feel, hear, see its movement. We know where it has come from—Antony's love of Caesar—and we know where it is going to. Now look at Hamlet. How do his soliloquies relate to the action of the play? Where do they come from? What happens as a result of them? Do his words lead to action? And is there action in the words?

In Hamlet's first scene he says nothing at all for over sixty lines. He makes a few cryptic comments when Claudius speaks to him, is persuaded not to go back to Wittenberg after defending his mourning in a rather flowery speech, and then is left alone. We know very little about him as he starts:

> O, that this too, too solid flesh would melt,
> Thaw and resolve itself into a dew…

We are plunged inside a mind. There is no obvious dramatic preparation. But the fact that he has been sitting saying nothing, that he has been so hidden in his dialogue with his uncle/father and aunt/mother, must hide a preparation. We want to know what is behind the silence. The first thing he tells us is that he would rather not be, to have the responsibility of being. He speaks of suicide but doesn't say why; it's an idea he has already rejected. He makes a generalised statement about his feelings and then uses a metaphor about the state of Denmark. Cryptically he says, 'That it should come to this!' What 'it' and what 'this'? In spasms of emotion, expressed in broken phrases and interjections, we learn very slowly of his mother's remarriage. It takes him the whole speech to voice the word 'married'. He compares his uncle to his dead father, comments on the speed of the remarriage, describes his parents' relationship, but not in logical sequence. We have moved from generalisation to the painfully specific; the rottenness of Denmark as a metaphor both for his state of mind and the life round him. The movement of the speech is disjointed and searches for an outcome that it cannot possibly find. It tells us no new facts but makes us part of an unresolved journey. Hamlet works through the situation without deciding on any course of action and finishes:

> But break, my heart, for I must hold my tongue.

The wave breaks, the waters retreat. This kind of cyclic movement establishes the rhythm of the play. The action has not moved forward, but its not moving is part of the true action of the play. The soliloquy has taken us from the social, external situation of affairs of state to an individual's feelings, and we know the conflict between the two will make the stuff of the play.

The soliloquy at the end of the scene with the Ghost has to carry the impact on Hamlet of what has been revealed by his father, and he nearly cracks in the impossibility of the task. Again there is the long build-up in which Hamlet is only listening, with just three or four violent interjections to the inexorable narrative of the Ghost. As he is left alone he is almost incoherent in the attempt to release his feelings.

> O all you host of heaven! O earth! What else?
> And shall I couple hell?

Unlike the 'solid flesh' speech, which is the accumulation of a feeling over a longer period of time, this is hot from the moment, immediate, violent, produced by what he has just heard. The fulfilment of the scene is in the speech. This is akin to opera, when the narrative arrives at a point where the action stops and the emotion is released in an aria. In a play the action doesn't stop. The emotional reaction to what has happened is bound up with what is going to happen next. The tension is never fully released as it is in opera. It spurts out jaggedly:

O most pernicious woman!
　[His first thought is not of the murder or the
　murderer but of the adulterous mother]
O villain, villain, smiling damnèd villain!
　[Not the crime but the hypocrisy]
My tables, my tables, meet it is I set it down
　[He actually writes down his thoughts]
That one may smile and smile and be a villain.
At least I'm sure it may be so in Denmark.
　[He finishes writing]
So, uncle, there you are. Now to my word:
It is 'Adieu, adieu, remember me.'
I have sworn't.

But what has he sworn? To remember the Ghost? Not one
word of murder or revenge, though both words have been
used dominantly in the scene with the Ghost. We, with
Hamlet, are off balance. What happens next is the scene of
the 'wild and whirling words' and the swearing to silence of
Horatio and Marcellus with the Ghost under the stage. But
even the swearing does not resolve the scene as Hamlet
shifts his ground to escape from the power, perhaps evil
power, of the Ghost. The physical image is of wild and
uncertain action and the scene ends with:

The time is out of joint. O cursèd spite
That ever I was born to set it right.

What his next action will be is unclear, but the speech has
taken us forward in some sense. Something is about to
happen.

The next soliloquy comes at the end of the long and complex second scene of Act 2. It includes, among other things,
the antic dialogue with Polonius, the arrival of Rosencrantz
and Guildenstern, in the middle of which we have 'What a
piece of work is a man', and then the arrival of the Players.
The metaphor of the stilled action of Pyrrhus's sword and
the theatrical emotion of the First Player in the Hecuba
speech provide the themes of 'O, what a rogue and peasant

slave am I' at the end of the scene. Hamlet reviews his own behaviour as if he were an actor performing, rather than a man who has to act. He feels his emotions, rather than his actions, have been inadequate. He works himself up into a frenzy—

> Bloody, bawdy villain;
> Remorseless, treacherous, lecherous, kindless villain!
> O, vengeance!

like a very bad actor—something he realises immediately, pulls himself together in a very upper-class way ('Steady, Carruthers, behaving like a tart on a Saturday night'), and produces, apparently from nowhere, the idea of *The Mousetrap*.

> The play's the thing
> Wherein I'll catch the conscience of the King.

And the act ends as theatrically and decisively as one could wish. At last he is prepared for action. Or so we think.

Fifty-five lines later he is on stage saying, 'To be or not to be.' The odd thing about the most famous speech in dramatic literature is that it is so undramatic. It doesn't come from anywhere. All the other soliloquies occur when Hamlet is already on the stage in a situation and what he says has a relationship to what has gone before. In this, Hamlet just walks onto the stage and starts the speech. He may enter very slowly and walk down centre stage like Jack Benny in the Lubitsch film, *To Be or Not To Be*, or he may bound on from the wings to get it over as soon as possible like Michael Pennington at Stratford. Or the director can build up to it with music and discover Hamlet at the top of the tower, dagger in hand, as Olivier did in the film, or reveal him in a hole in the ground, as Zeffirelli did in his stage production. But there is always the question of why he says it now and what has happened immediately before to make him say it.

However we interpret the meaning of the speech itself, we cannot relate it to the previous moment of apparent certainty. How has he got to this point? If he has had doubts he hasn't said so. The tenor of the speech is calm, dispassionate, not subjective or personal, which is wholly untypical of the Hamlet we have seen before. The extra syllable at the end of the first four lines gives it a heavy quality. It may or may not be about suicide but, even if it is, the suicide is not imminent. The first-person singular is not used once in the whole speech. It feels as if Hamlet is speaking not of his own situation but of a generalised philosophical problem. He even says, 'From whose bourn No traveller returns,' which he of all people knows to be untrue. The speech is so unrelated to anything that happens that it could easily be cut. If you didn't know it was Hamlet's—and the world's—most famous speech, no one would notice. In the 'bad' First Quarto the equivalent speech comes much earlier, so there is no break between the idea of catching the conscience of the King and its realisation. Since this version, however imperfect, must represent an actual performance, we can assume that actors at the time also realised the inconsistency and had corrected it as best they could. The First Quarto gives us an idea of the contemporary actors trying to make sense of a play by editing it and simplifying its meaning. It tries to iron out inconsistencies.

When I last directed the play at RADA in 1998, in a very cut version of the Second Quarto, I tried placing 'To be or not to be' in the earlier position. But it means you have the 'nunnery' scene and the rejection of Ophelia much earlier too, which feels wrong. The soliloquy becomes a loose cannon disturbing the balance wherever it is put. The speech represents a point of stasis in the play in which nothing happens, a still centre in which even Hamlet's turbulent mind is relatively calm. This is not a very satisfactory interpretation. It goes no way to explaining its meaning. Its fascination may partly be its lack of dramatic logic, as if

Shakespeare is taking off into an entirely new way of looking at what makes a play. The action has to proceed, Claudius has to be killed, the mayhem will happen, but at the centre of the play is a non-action. This could be the beginning of the road to *Godot*.

Hamlet's only other major soliloquy is at the end of the scene with the captain when he is on his way to England with Rosencrantz and Guildenstern.

> How all occasions do inform against me
> And spur my dull revenge.

This is by far the most coherent, reasoned and purposeful of all the solo speeches. It is not printed in the Folio and must have been dropped, possibly for reasons of length, but the play is overlong anyway and there are many much less interesting passages left intact. The speech feels almost as if Shakespeare is trying to get the play back on course by giving Hamlet a clear sense of purpose, even if no plan of action. But it is peculiarly placed. He has had his chance after the play scene and completely blown it. Now he is under armed guard and on his way to exile, which makes nonsense of his saying:

> I do not know
> Why yet I live to say 'This thing's to do',
> Sith I have cause and will and strength and means to
> do't

when he so patently doesn't have the means. He leaves the stage saying:

> My thoughts be bloody or be nothing worth!

In fact we don't see him again until the graveyard scene. In the interim he has disposed of Rosencrantz and Guildenstern, his most practical, prepared and coolly executed action in the whole play, but one we only hear about from his own mouth. When he comes back from England he is a different man. Apart from the outburst over Ophelia's grave he is resigned, detached and purposeful. He has arrived at action offstage.

When I was preparing the RADA production of the play I was scribbling away using words and sketches to make sense of the play's progression, not a storyboard of stick men and women acting out incidents, but a visual diagram of the forward movement of the play. I found I had made three columns down the page something like this:

Act One, Scene One	Act One, Scene Two	Act One, Scene Three
The Battlements	The Court	Polonius's Home
Soldiers and the Ghost	King and Queen	Polonius's Family
Hamlet (Supernatural/ Political)	Hamlet (Political/ Domestic)	Hamlet (Domestic/Social)
	Hamlet and Horatio	

Act One, Scene Four

The Battlements

Hamlet, the Soldiers and the Ghost

End of first movement

Some things were already clear. The action was far from linear like the action of *Oedipus* or *Rosmersholm*. Their narratives could be shown in one column in straight progression (apart from the choruses in *Oedipus*). In a classic play, the revelations of Horatio to Hamlet in Scene 2 should drive on to the scene on the battlements. Instead we have the leisurely scene of Polonius's precepts to his son and the commands to Ophelia to return her letters to Hamlet. We have to focus on another set of characters and wait to see what happens when Hamlet meets the Ghost. Like a second subject in sonata form, the Polonius household has to make its statement before the first can be developed.

By the end of Act I the themes of the play are already in place: Hamlet's reaction to his father's death and mother's remarriage, Ophelia's love for and forced separation from Hamlet, the country on the brink of war. The Ghost comes crashing in with his revenge theme and jolts the action forwards (or not, as it turns out). Looked at visually, the three-way lateral spread of the play pulls against and slows down the linear progression of incidents. The tension between them is part of the action. There are thematic parallels between the columns of which the most immediate is the child/parent relationship: Hamlet with his surrogate father and real mother, Ophelia with her father, Hamlet with his real but ghostly father. I was reminded of *King Lear*, where the double plot is more obviously part of the structure of the play: two old men with their children; Lear with his daughters and Gloucester with his sons.

I went on with the analysis, which was nowhere near as neat as the above layout suggests. My diagram was full of squiggles and arrows and sketches of people in corridors. Hamlet appeared in the interstices between the columns, peering round corners. When I came to work on the set with my co-director Henk Schut, the three columns became translated into physical terms. The play was set in three separate mini-auditoriums, side by side, in the same room, two audiences facing one way and one the other. Each audience faced a different small stage, which was a box with three sides in which the more intimate domestic scenes were played. Each was only completely visible to one-third of the audience, but the action of each stage was monitored by cameras and transmitted on screens to the other two. There was a large central area, visible to the whole audience, in which all the major ensemble scenes were played. Sometimes scenes would expand into this central area. This was not a scheme rigidly followed through, but it did create the peculiar atmosphere of the play, which is private and domestic on one hand and political and universal on the other. The exclusion of direct vision and the monitoring of the scenes on camera sustained the image of surveillance which is so relevant to the play and our own overlooked society.

Did it work? Yes, some of the time, but like any production of *Hamlet* no conceptual idea will work if it cannot be dominated by the actor playing the part. You cannot reduce the Prince of Denmark to a figure in a concept, and it was asking too much of the student actor to rise above it. But I liked the way the play's structure had been mirrored in its physical realisation.

5
Talking to the Audience

In a play how do you show those thoughts and feelings that a character cannot express to the other characters? The Elizabethans used soliloquy and in the hands of Shakespeare it became a major element of the play. But how did they do it at the Globe? Did the actor talk directly to the audience? Did he acknowledge their existence all the time?

In the case of Richard III and Iago, comedy villains who are letting us in on their wicked schemes, the answer is, clearly, 'Yes'. The characters demand a complicity from the spectators, so that the audience will enjoy the fruition of the schemes. The actors have the direct contact of the stand-up comedian. But what about speeches of introversion, where the character meditates on his situation? Like the 'Upon the king...' soliloquy in *Henry V*. Olivier in the film version attempted to make the convention acceptable to a modern audience by putting his voice on the soundtrack but not moving his lips. He tried to think the lines into the camera, which made for very boring cinema and very bad theatre. We felt cheated, not by the lack of contact but by a lack of sensual fulfilment. We needed to see the actor speaking in order to feel the emotion; to feel his words travel to us. The art of opera is based on this premiss. (Singers look ridiculous in close-up on television because their voice is geared to travel the distances of a theatre.)

This need is one of the basic givens of the theatrical experience. It does not necessarily mean that the character is in direct communication with us or that he acknowledges the audience as he speaks.

Peter Hall is quite clear about what he thinks:

> Every soliloquy is a public debate with the audience. Hamlet's 'To be or not to be' is a challenge to the audience. Three thousand people in daylight would never have their attention held by an actor privately communing with himself. The argument, shape and vocabulary of every soliloquy demands the direct participation of the audience.

> *(Exposed by the Mask)*

And what is meant by direct participation? Does the audience heckle Hamlet in the middle of his speech or argue points with him? 'To be or not to be, that is the question.' 'No, it isn't, mate, why don't you just do something?' It would be fun... once. Does the actor make individual eye contact with members of the audience, inviting them to answer back? If he is looking at one person he is excluding everyone else. Even when I am giving a lecture I will speak to a generalised unit, a group with whom I want to communicate, not to individuals. And in a lecture I am in the same space and time as the audience. An actor in a play creates a situation in another time and space; he knows the audience is watching him but this makes the imaginative leap more bold. If he admits he is in the here and now of his audience, he ceases to be in the there and then of Elsinore. Sometimes there are moments, as in the Chorus in *Henry V*, where the actor is in the same time and space as the audience:

There is the playhouse now, there must you sit.

But he is very soon demanding that we work on our imaginary forces. Being drawn in to another time, another place is surely one of the basic elements of theatre. So is the entering of the mind of another person, to understand their struggles and their innermost thoughts. Does anyone really believe that 'O, that this too, too solid flesh would melt' is delivered in the same way as 'Now is the winter of our discontent'?

The advocates of the 'in yer face' soliloquy are those whose fantasy of Elizabethan theatre is one of orange-wenches selling their wares, and actors bellowing at the groundlings in crude and robust plays. Brecht wondered why Olivier in his film of *Henry V* presented the acting of Shakespeare's company as more vulgar than his own. Brecht himself was to suffer under directors and actors who thought 'Brechtian' was another term for English pantomime, with the actors constantly dropping out of character and acknowledging the audience. Anyone who saw his production of *Mother Courage* will know this is nonsense. Nothing could have been more concentrated and serious, nor further from traditional popular entertainment. (Perhaps that's why Joan Littlewood had so little sympathy with his theatre.)

The altering of the awareness of time is the first step to the understanding of an action. If we are all chugging along in the same boring workaday world why are we in the theatre at all? We need to believe in the otherness of time and space to be able to enlarge the perception of our own lives. Brecht would have seen this as a typically bourgeois concept: the need to escape to another world to avoid looking at our own world and changing it. But all Brecht's plays are parables using the past. He insists by projected titles that we are very precisely in the Thirty Years War or Galileo's Rome in 1633, and by looking at those societies come to understand our own. We always know we are in a theatre but our degrees of empathy, of character involvement, will vary. I have always thought that the lessons of Brecht were rather wasted in Britain where the tendency of audiences is to stand outside the action and see the comic side of even the most pitiable situation. I first became aware of this when I went to a matinee of *A Streetcar*

Named Desire in Manchester, when Stanley's treatment of Blanche provoked gales of ribald mirth.

This may be another example of 'No sex, please, we're British'. Ever since the Puritan Revolution, British drama has been concerned with the concealment rather than the expression of emotion, at least in those plays that are good enough to have survived—mainly comedies. This progressive interiorisation of emotion has lasted to Coward and Pinter. The aside in Restoration Comedy is more complex because the connection with the audience is brief, but is never introvert. In a recent production of *The Man of Mode* by George Etherege I foolishly cut the asides, until I found that they carried the emotional life of the characters. The play is principally concerned with the obsession of a monied class with social behaviour, the displaying of wit and the clothes they wear. If and when they feel something stronger it is concealed from the other characters and they tell us in asides: the open expresssion of emotion was thought unstylish and courted ridicule.

With the coming of the proscenium stage, the soliloquy dwindled into the aside and it has gone on dying ever since. The semi-illusory nature of the late-nineteenth-century realistic theatre and the completely illusory nature of the cinema, where we sit privately in the darkness and identify with the characters, made audiences expect a more naturalistic presentation of private thoughts. The soliloquies in Chekhov's *The Seagull* now sound artificial and are sometimes, mistakenly, cut. In the twentieth century the device was resurrected in O'Neill's *Strange Interlude*, where the characters speak not only their dialogue but their thoughts as well, which makes for a very long and boring evening. It was wonderfully mocked by Groucho Marx in *Duck Soup*.

I once did a promenade production of *Macbeth* (RADA, 1996) in a small space. The audience were pressed up against the actors even in the most violent and intimate scenes. If anything, the actors' concentration on maintaining their situation, their space and time, against the palpable existence of the spectators was even stronger. At no point did they make eye contact or communicate with actual members of the public. There was a strange sense of existing in double space and time. Perhaps that is always true even in the darkened auditorium of the proscenium theatre, but it is just more strongly felt in the round and even more so in a promenade production.

There was an unusual variant of this in *The Speakers*, a version of Heathcote Williams's book about Speakers' Corner in Hyde Park, which Max Stafford-Clark and I directed for the Joint Stock Theatre Group in 1974. At the opening of the play we are in a recreation of Hyde Park, with speakers on soapboxes in different corners of the space, competing for our attention. The audience is free to wander between them. The light over the whole area is even, there is no illusion. The act of imagination has already taken place. The audience have tacitly agreed to be the listeners at Speakers' Corner in Hyde Park; they are already in the imagined world of the actors, who look at them and speak to them directly but as people in the speakers' world. As the play progresses we move into the private lives of the individual speakers, controlled by the lighting which ceases to be general and shrinks down to smaller and smaller areas, even to a solo spot on an actor's face. And then it opens out again and we are back in the park. The audience moves between the psychology of the individual to the social situation and back again, controlled in our time by the lighting operator, in Shakespeare's time by the movement of the writing. 'Now I am alone…' Hamlet says and the spotlight narrows, we are in his mind. Horatio and Bernardo appear and it opens out.

Another variation on the question of audience address was in my adaptation of Raymond Carver's story *Cathedral*. The story is told in the first person by an unnamed man. He tells how his wife brought home a blind man with whom she had worked and had a special relationship. The blind man arrives and after the wife has gone to bed the two sit listening to the television together. There is a programme about cathedrals and the storyteller tries and fails to communicate to the blind man what a cathedral is. The blind man persuades him to draw a cathedral, which the man does first with his eyes open and then with his eyes shut.

In the adaptation the actor tells the story directly to the audience and two other actors play the wife and the blind man. The story is played out with dialogue but the storyteller continues the narrative throughout, interspersed with his own thoughts. Although the story is in the past tense the action is in the present, and so, in a sense, is the narration. There is no sense of memory, of something recollected; it is all here and now. The man, without knowing it, describes his own voyage of discovery. By his own admission he has no feeling for poetry and when questioned admits he has no religious belief. By the end of the story he has experienced something akin to both, but he never tells us this. The writing is spare and unemotional, yet we understand everything. The actor maintains the inner life of the character while communicating with an audience. He is not inviting comment or even sharing an attitude; he is just telling us a story.

A story is something that has already happened and is told in the past tense. A play is something that has the pretence of happening here and now, but we know we are watching a story that has already been completed in the writer's mind, and that the ritual will be repeated the following night. In the theatre we live in the present and the past. The actor should be in charge of the audience's experience and must make decisions as to how far he wants them to enter his inner state and how far to remain detached. There is no simple answer.

6
Stage Directions

How far does a dramatist visualise his work on the stage as he writes it? Does he see his characters existing and moving in a stage space as they speak the dialogue? Did Shakespeare imagine the actor in the inn yard or on the platform at the Globe or at Blackfriars? The idea of a fixed physical shape for a theatre was new. Shakespeare was an actor and a shareholder in the company, and he knew he was bound by physical and economic restrictions. He had to be flexible, and he specifies little. His plays need practically nothing—a balcony in *Romeo and Juliet*, a grave in *Hamlet*, and that's about it. His stage directions are few but very specific. '*The Ghost of Banquo enters and sits in Macbeth's seat.*' You don't get much more specific than that. In his last plays he was lured or pressured into scenic effects. When I directed *Cymbeline* at Stratford in 1962 I fulfilled to the letter the stage direction '*Jupiter descends on an eagle.*' An actor descended from the flies on an eagle whose wings covered the stage. It had never been done like that in recent memory (as with all spectacle, people liked it for the wrong reasons). There are also many directions embedded in the text itself. The Ghost in *Hamlet* should be in full armour with his visor raised, moving 'slow and stately', and may have a field marshal's baton. All that is indicated in the speeches of the play as precisely as any stage direction. When did you last see them fulfilled in a production of *Hamlet*?

Even when plays moved back behind the proscenium arch there was no attempt to represent the detailed reality of everyday life. There was no furniture to speak of—look at the print of Molière sitting on one solitary chair centre stage in *Le Malade imaginaire*. Plays were still basically made up of dialogue spoken on a platform. Only by the end of the nineteenth century was there an attempt to put real rooms on the stage. In *Three Sisters* thirteen people sit down to a meal. In Granville Barker's *The Voysey Inheritance* a large fully set dining table dominates much of the action. Sometimes Barker got carried away, as if he were writing a novel; at the end of the first act of *The Madras House* he sends the characters offstage to a Sunday lunch which he describes in detail but which obviously was never meant to be seen. But Barker was directing his own play and knew what he was doing. This move towards detailed realism reached its fullest statement in the work of Stanislavsky and Nemirovich-Danchenko at the Moscow Art Theatre. Chekhov was not a man of the theatre and depended on his directors for the productions of his plays, however much he disagreed with them. His dislike of Stanislavsky's sound effects is well known. This division between actor and director has been a strong element in theatre since that time.

The case of Beckett is interesting: a writer who came late to playwriting after a series of novels, with no knowledge of theatre, and writing in French, which was not his own language. To begin with he was content to let Roger Blin direct his plays in Paris. Later he directed all his own plays in Germany, though not their first production. The physical settings of Beckett's plays are never in doubt. The tree in *Godot* is bare in the first act, in the second it has a leaf; Winnie is buried up to her waist in Act 1 of *Happy Days* and up to her neck in Act 2; the three characters in *Play* are in urns up to their necks; *Not I* is just a mouth talking, spotlit in darkness. The existence of the characters in their imprisonment intensifies their verbal presence. In his later plays his stage directions became more precise and more demanding on the skills of the actor. There are famous stories of him debating the number of steps to be taken in *Footfalls*. In the plays he has left a straitjacket for the director which it is difficult to break out of without losing the experience of the play.

Sometimes in my obsession with honouring a writer's text, and perhaps because I was scared to commit myself to interpretation, I have based my production too closely on an existing model. Brecht had all his own productions recorded photographically, moment by moment, and kept in a model book as a guide for future revivals. When I came to direct *Mother Courage* at the Old Vic in 1965 I followed the model book very closely. I admired the Berliner Ensemble production more than anything I had seen in the theatre—and still do—and I could not see how it could be improved on. I argued that every moment of the grouping on the stage had been looked at and altered many times until the right dialectical statement had been arrived at. Which may have been true, but, when we tried to reproduce it, it made for a lifeless show. We had not made our own search. It is said that Brecht's actors were not really part of the process either. Observers describe how Brecht would sit in the stalls with his designers and large numbers of assistants who discussed each moment, making sketches and moving the actors like chessmen. If you have very tough and talented actors who will accept such a method, it can work. But it is not the British way.

Brecht was directing a play which he had written many years before. It was premiered in Zurich during the war, not directed by Brecht. After the war, Brecht returned to Berlin and chose *Courage* to inaugurate his new company in 1949. He directed the play from the point of view of his theory, which he had developed over the years, but which, in exile, he had little opportunity to put into practice, apart from the

Galileo with Charles Laughton, which Brecht and Jo Losey directed in New York. Beckett's plays were performed soon after they were written; the physical elements of the production were not involved during rehearsal but are embedded in the text. Brecht may always have imagined Courage pulling her wagon against the movement of the revolving stage and so staying in the same place (an idea he had pinched from his contemporary, Erwin Piscator) but there are other ways of doing it: for instance, when you don't have a revolving stage. In *Happy Days* Winnie is buried up to her waist in Act 1 and to her neck in Act 2. If, as a director, you can't accept that, you can't do the play. Every line in the plays is based on those given circumstances. They limit the director and the actors but there is nothing you can do about it. Recently Peter Brook directed an evening of short plays by Beckett, including *Rockaby*. In *Rockaby* a woman sits in a rocking chair, rocking to and fro as she talks. In Brook's production, Kathryn Hunter stood behind the chair and tilted it backwards and forwards with her hands. I found this perverse and wilful. If she is not in the chair there is no play. I believe that Brook starts by giving the actor—or himself—a complete freedom to start from scratch. It's an approach that can produce interesting work, but does not necessarily end up where the author wanted, or make as powerful a statement as it could. The actor's work has been arrived at by chance or impulse. The writer has formulated something very strong, already completed. In Brecht's case, a political statement; in Beckett's, a poetic/musical image. With both writers, the actor has to find his own freedom, his own dynamic life, within a prescribed form. It's a director's job to help him. It may well be that Beckett had too strict an idea of the form of his plays, both physical and temporal, and this may affect their future life—though not I think that of *Godot* or *Endgame*. The terrible example of the productions of the D'Oyly Carte Opera, which went on presenting the Gilbert and Sullivan operas exactly as Gilbert had directed them, long after the poor man was dead, is a warning against all over-reverent reconstructions of the past. But I doubt that Beckett can survive a radical rethink without ceasing to exist, and cosmetic tinkering by jazzing the plays up with red noses and banging drums is just crass.

I am like any other director or actor. I want elbow room, space in which my imagination can work, or at least my craft. Directing Beckett is stimulating as a discipline, and can be more, but I wouldn't want to do it all the time. Recently I have turned to adaptations of non-dramatic work, where I can feel that I am truthful to the spirit of the writer but can create my own theatrical form. I hope this is more honest than taking a play whose theatrical life is already articulated and laying my alternative on top.

How far writers of our own time visualise the physical realisation of their work became clear in some work at RADA. I was directing a selection of scenes with second-year students, not for public showing and with token staging, in 2007. The scenes were by Beckett, Pinter, Edward Bond, Caryl Churchill and Peter Gill, all writers with some elements in common: spare, sometimes cryptic, dialogue; simple staging demands; and concealed rather than exposed emotion. They represent a cross-section of the last fifty years or so of drama. Apart from Beckett all the writers were British and, at that time, still alive. Some of them were my personal friends (Pinter, Churchill and Gill), although I had not directed their work professionally. Bond was the writer closest to me: I had directed the first productions of his early work. The plays were Beckett's *All That Fall*, Pinter's *Old Times*, Bond's *Saved*, Churchill's *A Number*, and Gill's *Small Change*.

All That Fall is a radio play and was written to be heard only, as dialogue and sound effects. Beckett was very strict about not allowing it to be staged, though many tried to persuade him, including Laurence Olivier and Joan Plowright. Which is a pity because the play is more accessible, more naturalistic and funnier than most of the plays he wrote for the stage. The excerpt we worked on involved the return journey of the Rooneys from the railway station, Mrs Rooney leading her blind husband. Most of the physical stage images are created by the sound effects—the train, the donkey braying, the snatch of Schubert, and the dragging footsteps which seem to prefigure *Footfalls*. It's a relatively easy job to give it a physical life, though it may not have had the presence that Beckett would have wanted. In our adaptation the stillness of the Rooneys when they stop and the old man looks in the ditch, had as much presence as the stage plays. Will they get home, reach the end of their journey, or will they die on the way? Death we shall not see nor hear, only the sound of the dragging footsteps fading away. Beckett shows us a man and woman on the journey of life, a section of which we are allowed to see, that started before the play began and will go on after it is finished. Time may be an illusion, but we experience the action as happening in time. The past and the future and the world outside are ambiguous but the onstage life has a reality.

A year later I managed to persuade the Beckett estate to let me do a full stage production of *All That Fall* (RADA, 2008). The staging demands were the cart and the hinny pulling it, the bicycle, the car, the steps at the station, the train and the journey of the two old people. I was fortunate to have the collaboration of Toby Sedgwick, the inspired movement creator. The cart was made by four actors with a bridle, a plank and two skeleton wheels, the bike was just the handlebars, the car was four plain kitchen chairs, the steps were mimed. The arrival of the train was created by the lighting designer, Neal Fraser, and the sound department. Their work had all the charm of improvisation though it was very carefully choreographed, and in no way detracted from the intensity of the writing. I can't believe that Beckett would not have liked it. It worked partly because the audience took great pleasure in the make-believe, that particular ability of the theatre to show you how things are done at the same time as you accept what they are meant to be. This never attracted Beckett. I think his process of imagining was more that of a poet or a visual artist. Theatre, in the sense of communicating and adapting to a live audience, did not interest him. But I did not think any of the physical realisation of the sounds detracted from the intensity of the words or the atmosphere of a radio play. I felt we had been completely faithful to the text with enough freedom to feel creative in our own contribution.

Pinter's characters in *Old Times* have conflicting stories of their past lives but, unlike Beckett's, are imprisoned by their relationship rather than dictated to by forces outside themselves. The physical demands of furniture and properties (coffee, brandy, cigarettes) are those of any play of the Noël Coward era, the essentials of any repertory production in the 1950s, when Pinter first worked as an actor. He imagines a recognisable physical environment but pared down to essentials; the demands on a designer are minimal. The action is as continuous in each act as in any traditional play. The characters are working through their relationships in present time by recounting a conflicting and ambiguous past. The reality of the play exists in the present emotional conflicts of which the dialogue is the guard, the concealment. This too may stem from Coward's *Private Lives* where Elyot and Amanda talk about Norfolk, the Taj Mahal, and the Duke of Westminster's yacht to conceal the reawakening of their emotional life. In Pinter's *Old Times* the sexual relationship of the man and the two women is presented through conflicting stories of a visit to the cinema to see *Odd Man Out*.

Peter Gill's *Small Change* is about two Welsh working-class Catholic boys struggling to define their relationship. Nothing is resolved, and the narrative, though often violent, has little sense of forward motion. It is kaleidoscopic, shifting backwards and forwards in time and place, sometimes in the same scene, but I do not feel that the physical life on the stage is inherent in the text. There are too many areas of ambiguity. The tension varies without apparent cause. The specific location of any one scene is not important. It is difficult to feel the presence or the action. Gill's later play *The York Realist* takes place in a totally realistic environment (a farm kitchen) and, for me, is a more successful piece of work. Gill gives no stage direction in his early plays but he usually directs the first production himself and appears to know exactly how he will stage them. He uses a few identical plain wooden chairs in space, and explores their potential to the limit. But I feel the stage image that he creates with such certainty as a director is not apparent in the words on the page.

Caryl Churchill sets her later plays in recognisable environments but does not describe them. It does not seem important to her how they are realised in physical terms. She is, to me, the least sensual of the writers and I feel that some of her later plays like *A Number* are not imagined for the stage. *A Number* could be staged realistically and would lose little in the process; in fact it might gain. Plain chairs on a bare wooden floor have become one of the clichés of contemporary theatre, and they are now a convenience rather than an essential visual element. They save the designer from having to define the social background. If the play is very powerful we don't mind too much, but it can conceal a kind of laziness. Many writers—and Churchill is certainly not one of them—write plays as if for television, moving the location with every short scene and ignoring the responsibility of the physical restrictions of theatre. In the process, directors have evolved more and more ingenious presentation of scene changes. With Churchill's plays the problem is not one of solving difficult questions of staging but finding a setting and a physical life which are right for the play without distorting it. Her next play after *A Number* (*Drunk Enough to Say I Love You?*) was staged in a black void; the two characters sat on a sofa which levitated off the floor as the play progressed. I found this an irritating idea, but it was not inherent in the play. It was an idea of the director, James Macdonald, which the writer had gone along with. A future production may well do the play differently. Interestingly, Macdonald had very successfully directed Sarah Kane's last play, *4.48 Psychosis*, which is more of a poem than a play. There are no stage directions and no indication of characters in the script she delivered a week before she killed herself. Macdonald had to make all the decisions about staging. He divided the text between three actors and, with his designer, evolved the idea of the action played on the floor reflected in a huge mirror over the stage. It was an effective realisation of a play that had no stage life in its text.

Edward Bond in his early plays has a very clear sense of where his scenes take place, and what the minimum essentials are to represent them. The second scene of *Saved* is set on a boating lake in South London. Len, who has picked up Pam and now lives in her parents' house, is rowing her on the lake. They speak of their future. It is the only scene in the play when the characters have a chance of happiness. The boatman calls them in and makes a play for Pam. The scene demands a full-size rowing boat, with oars, and nothing else. It is a real object but set without illusion in the stage space. If the scene were filmed realistically it would lose everything. When I first worked with Bond on the play he was quite specific as to how he saw objects on the stage down to the minutest detail, even the colour of a balloon. His stage may be minimally furnished, but it is a real world not an imaginary one. A world which has the possibility of change.

I directed *Saved* twice, once in its first production in 1965 and again in 1969 after we had succeeded in getting rid of the censor. It can be read as a perfectly naturalistic play about a family in South London. It is written in mainly one-line dialogue, but it has none of the mannered repetitions and patterning that characterise Pinter's work, and the narrative is not at all puzzling or cryptic. The structure, which is highly original, moves in a straightforward progression though the thirteen scenes, though there are time gaps in which there are considerable leaps in the action. The stage directions are spare, with an overall direction that *'The stage is as bare as possible—sometimes completely bare'*. Bond had absorbed the pattern of the staging based on Brecht that we used at the Royal Court and made his own version of it. Three of the scenes are in a park, one is in the prison, one in a café, the rest take place in the living room or the bedroom. It was Bond's idea that there should be only one door upstage set in a couple of angled flats which would serve as both living room and bedroom. The living-room furniture consisted of a table and two chairs, right, an armchair, centre, and a sofa, left, more or less in a line and facing front. There was no attempt visually to give it an atmospheric life. All the props and when they are to be used are indicated in the text.

The father and mother of Pam, have not spoken to each other for many years. In one scene the mother gets Len to mend her stocking while she is still wearing it, a scene both erotic and innocent. The father sees this and in a later scene the parents speak to each other in a violent and childish row, during which a chair leg accidentally comes loose. In the very last scene of the play the house has returned to its normal pattern of silent, loveless coexistence. There is no dialogue for the whole scene, which lasts several minutes, except one line from Len, who has decided to stay in the house though there is no reason why he should. He brings the broken chair on stage and says, 'Fetch me 'ammer,' but nobody moves. He mends the chair by himself. The action of each of the characters is described and has to be performed separately like a piece of music. The father is sitting at the table doing his pools, Pam and her mother sit on the couch facing front. In a series of precisely described movements Len fixes the chair leg and tests the stability. The last section of the scene reads like this:

> LEN *slips his left arm round the back of the chair. His chest rests against the side edge of the seat. The fingers of the right hand touch the floor. His head lies sideways on the seat.*
>
> MARY *sits.* PAM *sits.*
>
> HARRY *licks the flap on the envelope and closes it quietly.*
>
> *The curtain falls quickly.*

Bond claims it as an image of optimism: Len has mended the chair. The play is unique in using all the materials of naturalism but ordering the actions and controlling the timing so exactly that the statement is large and classic.

How far must a writer know what his plays will look like on the stage? Chekhov is a great writer for the theatre but knew little of stage practice—and yet the plays belong on the stage and translate with difficulty into other media. In film the director controls the focus, telling you what to look at. In a Chekhov play the spectator is free to decide where he looks among the people on stage. This sense of an equality among a group of characters, all of them interesting, is surely one of Chekhov's most revolutionary achievements and belongs essentially to the theatre. That he may not have known it was quite so original in no way detracts from his achievement.

When I start preparing a production I always work from the text outwards. What is in the text is essential to the performance of the play. I think I always understood this, but seeing the Berliner Ensemble, and then working with George Devine at the Royal Court and particularly with

Jocelyn Herbert, the designer, made it an absolute basis. Jocelyn was remarkable; she was the creator and guardian of the Royal Court style. Her whole career was centred in the work and purpose of that theatre. She was as equally at home with Brecht as she was with Beckett, whose chosen designer she became. Writers who knew little of the stage, but made huge demands on it, set her tasks for which she would always find the answer. Wesker's *The Kitchen*, with its cast of thirty kitchen staff, requires an entire kitchen with various stations for the different chefs, all of which had to be in the sight lines of the Royal Court's narrow stage. The first production was on a Sunday night and had no budget. The chef's stations were created with tea chests, covered in black material and arranged in a projecting angled form. The stage was stripped bare to the back wall. Andy Phillips, the lighting designer, hung his lamps over the set in exactly the same configuration as the onstage structure, and so created an individual style. When it was peopled by the waiters and the chefs in frenzied action it was thrilling—and beautiful.

The style that evolved was never minimalism for its own sake, bleak and without atmosphere. Jocelyn would find the beauty in the simplest things just as Helene Weigel had done with her props. Her designs for my production of Brecht's first play, *Baal*, were breathtaking: over twenty different locations, each one suggested by the barest means but created with loving care. ('*Red willows hanging down*' was one of them.) Many of her productions, such as Storey's *The Changing Room* and Wesker's trilogy, needed detailed naturalism, but somehow she found the poetic element in realism just as she would find realism in poetry. The combination of writer/director/designer was of a unique quality. The imagining and filling of the stage space was shared between Storey/Anderson/Herbert and Wesker/Dexter/Herbert to make a series of unforgettable pieces of ensemble work.

Most plays can be done perfectly adequately without scenery, though not without costume or props. A good dramatist will somehow know the potential of the physical life of his or her play without necessarily being able to describe it. Some writers—Alan Ayckbourn is a supreme example—know the theatre so well professionally that they have an exact idea of how the play will be on stage. But all writers want their words and actions to be unimpeded by the visual presentation.

7
Action for the Actor

There is an acting method called 'actioning' which is used and described by Mike Alfreds and Max Stafford-Clark, among others. During a close reading of the play, usually taking several days, the director works through the text with the actors. The actor has to describe aloud each line of his or her part as an action with a transitive verb. He or she announces the action in the first person—'I cajole', 'I implore', 'I reproach'—and then says the line to demonstrate the action he has described. The method has many virtues. It prevents the actor living inside himself in a search for character, it produces an outgoing energy towards the other actors, and it makes for a variety of expression and colour. It is used in conjunction with a statement of an objective for the whole scene as analysed by Stanislavsky.

Stanislavsky in his theory uses the word 'objective' to describe the character's search, the need that drives him or her to action. An objective may be expressed in a single line but it is more likely to develop over several lines, a whole speech, a section of a scene or the entire scene. It may well not go forward in a straight line. The exploration of the objective gives you a 'through-line', a dynamic, which makes you feel free to explore the forward development of the action. The objective may change or be modified or blocked by the situation or the objectives of the other characters. (Stanislavsky thought the objectives were part of a larger movement he called the 'super-objective', though searching for this can be risky and misleading.) Actioning leads one into thinking of each line as a completed unit to be replaced by the next. And so in an intellectual sense it is. But an actor may feel his action as an unbroken movement moving through many lines of text. Making an action of each line tends to create a mechanical progression rather like those drawings where you join up numbered dots to reveal the hidden picture. There are no curves or bends; everything proceeds in straight lines. Most of all, it doesn't probe the intention of the action, it only describes the activity itself. With an objective, the energy goes beyond the end of the line and becomes part of the flow of the play. It is the identification with the intention, according to Stanislavsky, which gives the actor energy and truth.

Actioning is more valuable in the dialogue of a contemporary play than in a classic. It works least well in soliloquies. Unless you accept the gung-ho idea of talking directly to the audience, most soliloquies have no objects of a transitive verb. The method is inadequate to describe the movement of meditation or deliberation that is so essential to Shakespeare. He is concerned with the character's shift between his relation to the outside world and his communication with himself in response to that world. These shifts are not a conscious drive but more a response to a fluid situation. The best actors arrive at the modulation in a long speech by the ear in response to the text. By 'ear' I do not mean an awareness of the beauty of sound but an intuitive response to the emotional and intellectual moods expressed by the verbal shifts in the writing. The actor feels the changes and charts his or her way through it. This sounds vague and woolly compared to the methodical listing of actions, but the attempts I have seen to apply the actioning method to Hamlet's soliloquies destroyed the flow of the speech. The poetry had gone.

The shift between the inner and outer world is equally apparent in scenes of dialogue. In the second scene of *Twelfth Night* Viola has been shipwrecked. She enters the scene with the sailors who have rescued her.

VIOLA. What country, friends, is this?

CAPTAIN.   This is Illyria, lady.

VIOLA. And what should I do in Illyria?
My brother he is in Elysium.
Perchance he is not drowned. What think you sailors?

CAPTAIN. It is perchance that you yourself were saved.

VIOLA. O, my poor brother!—and so perchance may he be.

(Twelfth Night 1.2)

Viola's opening question to the sailors is a direct outward action. The second is reflective to herself, and is triggered by the name 'Illyria'. Viola responds to the name to make a pun in an emotional situation, a typical Shakespearean device. The ear is listening to the words before the emotion forms itself. The in/out movement is like the water in which her brother may or may not be drowned. Viola surfaces to ask another direct question and again the reply sends her back into herself; then she pulls herself out of the water and back into the play. I suggest that this process is a poetic one not easily described as conscious actions.

You can see it as the movement between transmitting and receiving. Actors often tend to see their part as a series of transmitting actions: nothing is received; there are no reactions. Playing the reaction to a line, a thought or a feeling is much more difficult for most actors than the transmitting. It is always easier for an actor to shout at his partner; he feels like he has done something, got somewhere, the blood runs through him, he goes red in the face: surely he is acting? As I say to my actors ten times a day: 'Anger is the easiest emotion to express. Find something else.' Great acting in the past was built round the moments of receiving and were usually silent—Irving hearing the bells which accuse him of his murder, Duse blushing when listening to a former lover, Garrick's start when he sees the Ghost of Hamlet's father. These were as consciously prepared as any action.

I am not an actor. I can only guess at how the process works. But I am certain of one thing: when you prepare your performance you don't decide how you will say each line. It is in the moment before you say the line, or more often a sequence of lines, that the acting happens. In this I am at one with the actioneers. In the moment the first word is said the direction and mood of a speech is already there, and moving. That moment cannot be expressed as a bare statement of a transitive verb and once the impulse, the action, if you like, is released it does not need more verbs to keep it alive. It has its own life and momentum.

Ken Tynan, in a moment of rare insight, described John Gielgud's approach to speaking in the words of Alexander Pope:

> The spider's touch, so exquisitely fine!
> Feels at each thread, and lives along the line.
>
> (*An Essay on Man*)

The actor creates an unbroken flow, even when there may be violent changes of mood or thought. The preparation may be a conscious focus on the events leading up to the moment in time—the given circumstances, the immediate pressure on the character—but then the energy is released. A long preparation, nothing, and then the action. An athlete on the starting blocks is not thinking 'I must win this race. I must be faster than the others.' He is not thinking anything and then he runs. I do not believe that if I am playing Hamlet and waiting for the King and the court to leave at the end of the second scene, that it helps to think 'I share with the audience my desire to be water,' or any other verbalisation you would care to offer of Hamlet's feeling at that particular moment.

Most of the chapters in this book are about getting to understand how the words of a play work, how they are used by the writer and how, therefore, they are useful to the actor. I do not claim to know how to act or how to teach anyone else to act. All methods are inadequate— Stanislavsky, Laban, Alexander, Suzuki. They offer partial insights but cannot give the actor his craft. Only experience will do that.

8
Action and Intention

CLOWN. For here lies the point: if I drown myself
wittingly, it argues an act, and an act hath three
branches; it is, to act, to do, and to perform.

(*Hamlet* 5.1)

The Clown/Gravedigger is trying to establish the truth
about Ophelia's suicide. Did she mean to drown herself?
Was she aware of her own actions?

CLOWN. Give me leave. Here lies the water—good.
Here stands the man—good. If the man go to the
water and drown himself, it is, will he nill he, he goes;
mark you that. But if the water come to him and
drown him, he drowns not himself. Argal, he that is
not guilty of his own death shortens not his own life.

Can an action be true without understanding the intention
of the character? Can you understand any action without
knowing where it is going? Or where it is coming from? In
the theatre the latter less than the former perhaps. We know
that Iago means to destroy Othello. The action of the play
is driven by his need to accomplish that destruction. We are
never completely satisfied by the reasons he gives: that he
has been passed over for the lieutenantship in favour of
Cassio, or that Othello may have slept with his wife, which
seems very unlikely. Coleridge famously called it 'motiveless
malignity'. The psychoanalysts tell us that Iago has an
unconscious homosexual passion for Othello, but though
an actor can colour his performance to convey this, the

focus of the actor must be on the 'What' rather than the 'Why'. For the audience the focus, the excitement, is on 'What is happening? How does he do it?' There must be a 'Why' to drive Iago to destroy Othello with such ruthlessness, but in the theatre we don't worry too much about it. Drama exists in the action that lies between the motivation of the past and the achievement of the future.

Can we detach action from motivation? Dr Johnson said:

> Moral good depends on the motive from which we act. If I fling half a crown at a beggar with the intention to break his head, and he picks it up and buys victuals with it, the physical effect is good; but with respect to me, the action is very wrong. In the same way, religious services, if not performed with an intention to please God, avail us nothing.

Johnson is not concerned with the character of the action, only its moral worth. In the theatre is the moral evaluation our prime concern? The actor is concerned with what he does. If an actor tried to demonstrate Johnson's example, the motivation would change the nature of the action. Throwing a coin to break the beggar's head is a different action from throwing it to feed him. If we imagine a third possibility—for example, I throw the coin to win admiration for my charity—we see that the action could be varied again. An actor could make this clear in performance. Acting is often concerned with just such refinements. The actor's search is how to define exactly the action itself, not to alter the emotional state. The Method people would disagree, arguing that the exact emotional state will produce the right action. I feel the actor must always be, to some extent, detached from his action.

The pressures of a situation on a character in Shakespeare could not, in themselves, produce the language he speaks. Imagine a Method preparation for Macbeth hearing of his wife's death. The director suggests the given circumstances:

'Your castle is surrounded by your own people, who hate you, and the English forces; you have no chance of escape; the wife who helped you seize the crown and on whom you were dependent but from whom you are estranged has gone mad. You hear a cry of women offstage. Someone tells you the Queen is dead. What do you say?' No actor in an improvisation is going to come up with 'She should have died hereafter, There would have been a time for such a word.' The words are given you by the writer. He has imagined something he wants the character to say, which may or may not be something he, the writer, wants to say. The actor has to find an attitude in which those words might be said. To do so he may have to get rid of the ego, the 'I', beloved of Stanislavsky, always difficult for the actor. He cannot force an interpretation on the speech.

An interesting example of action and intention occurred during my work on *The Caucasian Chalk Circle* (RSC, 1962). I begged a cigarette (it was in the days when we all smoked) from one of the actors and then asked the cast for descriptions of my action. All the answers given were concerned with the psychology of the individual, 'The actor is sucking up to you', etc. I pointed out that though this may have been an element, what happened in fact was an unremarkable social transaction based on the then low cost of the cigarette and not on our individual psychology. I used this as a starting point for analysing actions from the point of view of social and economic relationships in the play. Many years later, working on David Hare's *Fanshen* (Joint Stock, 1975), a play about the socialising of a group of peasants in a Chinese village, we took the analysis further—to the political outcome of the action. Not what the action was but what effect it had and what we, as actors, wanted to show by it.

When the Stanislavsky Method was adopted in America, actors tended to stress the Freudian elements, to analyse motivation rather than the outcome, political or otherwise.

This self-analysis, encouraged by the therapist/teacher and the therapist/director, developed the enormous egos of the Method actors, and contributed to their often very striking performances. It was usually based on Emotion Memory, a very limited part of the original Stanislavsky teaching. A more external actor like Olivier also splashed in the Freudian puddle in the 1930s. Under the influence of Tyrone Guthrie, the director, and Ernest Jones, the leading British Freudian of the time, he played Iago as sexually in love with Othello (without telling the Othello, Ralph Richardson), and his Hamlet had an Oedipus complex. Hamlet delays because he would like to have killed his father and made love to his mother. You see some traces of this in the film Olivier directed in 1948, with himself as Hamlet. The action takes place in a phallic tower at the top of which Hamlet meets the Ghost, says 'To be or not to be', and to which he is carried by the four soldiers at the end. But, for Olivier, a psychoanalytical approach was probably as external as, for instance, the dyed hair or false nose or Jewish accent which he adopted before he could start work on any part. He was a man of action; the future was always more important than the past; and this gave his performances their ruthless dynamic quality. He could create a sudden movement without any apparent preparation, as when he grabbed Tyrell's neck in the crook of his arm in *Richard III* and orders the murder of the two princes: 'Go, by this token.' It may have been a trick but it was also his absorption in the purity of action. It was the concentration of the athlete or the gymnast.

When he came to play Othello himself in 1964 he approached the part, as he always did, from the point of view of a man of action. He was remarkable in much of it, but there was a basic premise that he could never quite accept: that Othello is essentially passive to the actions of Iago and that the glory of the part is the richness of his emotional poetry in response to them. When he came to 'O now for ever Farewell the tranquil mind. Farewell content. Farewell the plumèd troops and the big wars That make ambition virtue. O farewell', he drove the speech to a kind of hysterical climax, clapping his hands like a sportsman on 'Othello's occupation's gone', driving the character to some future development, rather than bidding farewell to the past. Olivier in his own life cared little for the past; he was not nostalgic (unlike his rival Gielgud, who loved anecdotes about old actors), and he could not identify with a speech built on regret. Nor could we feel pity for the character in the situation. It needed the sad organ tones of Paul Robeson.

When you look at Shakespeare's tragic heroes most of them are responding to circumstances rather than creating them. Like the protagonists in Greek tragedy they delude themselves by thinking they are in charge of their destiny. True, Lear sets in motion the action which drives the rest of the play, but its greatness is in his moments of realisation. Only Coriolanus, the man of pure action, has no soliloquies and goes on no journey of self-awareness.

We look at action from the past and from the future. We ask, 'Why do you do this?'—either meaning, 'What in your past makes you do this now?' or 'What result do you hope to achieve in the future?' The first will tend to a psychoanalytic view of character, the second to a utilitarian approach. When Richard III woos Lady Anne what practical purpose does it serve for the future? To test his powers to manipulate others? There is no need in the narrative for him to marry Lady Anne; the play has not moved forward one inch by the end of it, but it's a great scene, the audience love being in on the villainy, and no one would ever dream of cutting it. It has a pure energy like the energy of clowns in a circus. He does it because he enjoys doing it. In the soliloquy at the end of *Henry VI, Part 3*, some of which Olivier interpolated into the first soliloquy of *Richard III*, Gloucester analyses the reason for his actions: 'Because I am so malformed I have no alternative outlet for my energy.' But it is commented on from the outside, not experienced as a mental torment and so Olivier played it.

Actors often say, 'My character wouldn't do that,' when, in fact, the excitement may come from the unexpectedness, the unpreparedness of the action. When Hedda shoots herself, Judge Brack says, 'But people don't do that sort of thing.' But she has; she is the exception which has exploded the rule. The action without apparent preparation is best seen in the martial arts. The fighters face each other and then the action happens. There is an emptying of the mind, the action and then nothing. I am told that in Japanese music one sound has to be completed before the next is made. It has to disappear into nothingness and come from nothingness.

I understood this most clearly when working on a production of *Hamlet*. I had decided to do the play in a bastardised version of modern dress, which is so usual today, and I was facing the problem of the swearing on the sword after the scene with the Ghost, which is so specific in the text. A sword strapped onto a modern suit looks ridiculous. My assistant on the production was the Japanese actress Noriko Barter, and I had the idea that she could be like the attendants in the kabuki theatre who, silently and without expression, change the actor's costume and hand him his props. Noriko would glide onto the stage, veiled in black, and hand Hamlet his sword. It worked, but it only worked because Noriko had no identity at all as she performed the action. She did not exist. It would have been much more difficult for most Western actors because the sense of 'this is me doing it' would have intruded.

The question all actors have to answer, though most of them don't know it, is, 'How willing am I to let the action of the play flow through me and how much do I want my ego, my personality to be felt?' The answer will always be different with each individual actor.

British actors, unlike American and some European actors, are inclined not to identify, not to commit themselves to the passion of a part. This may sometimes stem from a too great awareness of the writing. The revolution in acting started by the influence of Marlon Brando depends on a non-rhetorical sense; to live in the present and be unconscious of where the play is going. There is a breakdown of language as a formal expression. We are left with the immediate unshaped spurts of emotion. Brando faced huge problems when tackling the essentially rhetorical part of Antony in the film of *Julius Caesar* (though he is impressive and makes Gielgud, an excellent Cassius on the stage, seem very two-dimensional).

I am constantly dissatisfied with actors who are too *near* their text, who cannot hear the resonances of the writing, as if their words were only some form of emotional expression and did not relate to ideas—political, moral, religious, philosophical, poetic—which exist beyond the personal predicament of the character. I constantly ask actors not only 'What do you think? What do you feel?' but also 'What do you think about what you feel? What do you feel about what you think?'

It is tempting to think of a play as a piece of music. All you have to do is follow the composer's instructions and it will work. But it is never quite like that. However meticulously the writer lays out stage directions, pauses, tempo indications, there is always the moment when it has to be made flesh. In the beginning was the word and the word was with Sam Beckett, but it has to dwell amongst us. Beckett made the theatre of the second half of the twentieth century, but he was not part of it. In his later years he took to directing his own plays but he never saw a performance. He controlled every moment of his play but was not interested in the response of the live audience. Nor to a large extent are his actors. If you are the mouth in *Not I*, you are not going to play it differently if there are five hundred people in the audience or none. You won't know. I doubt that the Noh actor knows whether he has a good or bad house—the kabuki actor certainly does. It is interesting to see the audience at a performance of the Noh theatre in Japan; it is full of women in traditional kimonos who have studied the texts and follow it in their books while mouthing along with the actors, rather like cultists at *The Sound of Music.* There are no young people. It is still for me one of the great theatregoing experiences but only because my professional education has led me to appreciate it.

But I do believe that language, certainly in earlier periods, had a freedom that we have lost, and that it provided a richer and more complex experience. The movement towards greater realism, naturalism even, has brought the text physically nearer to the actor, sometimes disappearing down his throat in the mumbling of the Method. As a result it has become less open and universal. The increasing insistence on actual physical contact in all forms of acting, the use of microphones in the theatre, together with the experience of acting for camera, mean that is not necessary for the actor to open his or her throat and release the music. Some essential sensation of acting is lost.

9
Movement and Stillness—the Noh Theatre

I was rehearsing *Kinuta* (*The Fulling Block*), one of the Noh plays by the great fourteenth-century dramatist Zeami, at RADA in 1998. My co-director Henk Schut was teaching the actors the basis of the walk used in the Noh theatre, which he had learnt from a Noh actor. The walk consists of sliding first one foot and then the other along the floor without lifting either. The top part of the body is erect, the arms are held curved in front of the body, the knees are bent, the body is centred over the heels, eyes straight ahead. The feet are parallel and the transference of weight is imperceptible. The movement is endlessly sustained and forward. You have to wear socks and the floor has to be smooth. The actor moves heel to toe, and the toes lift a little off the ground as the foot reaches its forward position, but the movement is continuous. When performed correctly the walk creates energy and concentration but should appear effortless and light.

What does the walk express? That there is no beginning and no end; the actor is moving when we first see him, and he disappears moving. For a time he will live out the passion on the square we call the stage so we can see it and then he will leave. Most of the action will be in the mind. There will be no dead bodies to clear away as in the Elizabethan theatre, and no curtain to bring down. We, the audience, are outside time too. There is no exploration of motivation. Usually the first half of a Noh play is an action in the past involving living beings, the second is the consequence of the action, often a revisiting by a ghost of the main character.

The square wooden stage of the Noh theatre sits in the corner of the building; the audience sits on two sides of the square. Audience and performers are in the same space and the same lighting. The actors' approach to the stage is diagonally along a long walkway from the left at the back. The walkway is longer than the width of the stage itself, built of the same wood and fully visible to the audience. Strips of brightly coloured silk on bamboo are lifted to allow the actor to enter. He approaches the stage, fully masked in a heavy silk costume, with the sustained, even walk. It takes up to five minutes, but it can't be called slow. It is timeless. He is preceded by three musicians who play an important part in the play. They have a sung and chanted dialogue with the actors as well as establishing rhythms and sound with their instruments. The chorus who sit at the side enter from a lifted panel on the right-hand side and sit on the right in two rows. They do not use the sustained walk.

The stories of the plays are usually very simple. In *Kinuta* a government official leaves his wife to work in a distant city. The wife imagines she communicates with him by beating a fulling block (used for softening cloth), with her maid. The physical actions are minimally sketched by the movement of their fans; there is no sound. Eventually the wife dies of grief. In the second part her tormented ghost is finally calmed by the prayers of her husband. There is almost no narrative action and very little physical action of any kind. The actor is still for long periods, and when gesture is used it is very powerful. Most of the play is a Buddhist reflection on the torment of 'clinging': of being attached to desires that create pain, and the need to free oneself from desire. This is expressed by the intensity of the poetic and musical dialogue between the participants. The chorus and the musicians sometimes speak for the protagonist, sometimes he speaks for himself. Sometimes he performs a slow dance, again with minimal gesture, while the musicians and chorus chant. The sense of being rooted to the stage is a metaphor for the human imprisonment in its own karma. It can be very powerful or very boring, depending on whether you want to enter the world of a different theatre, a different philosophy and a different awareness of time.

If the audience does want to, its perceptions are sharpened. Everything that happens on the stage becomes important and meaningful. In Japan the actors are trained for years by older actors until they are ready to play the part. We rehearsed the play for five weeks with a group of untrained students. There was a small combined chorus of musicians and singers at the side using our own invented instruments—only percussion, no wind, no strings. It should have been laughable. In fact the concentration we shared in the process did communicate something in performance. Our anchor was the walk itself, which was rehearsed religiously before every performance, followed by a period of meditation in which the actor faces the wall in the same position, arms curved, knees lightly bent and the heels lifted just off the ground. Very demanding but focusing. The concentration on the minimalisation of the theatre event is a great head-clearer. I felt I had understood it in some form all my life but I was now experiencing it.

I have always been fascinated by the idea of stillness in the theatre, or nearly always. My first student productions were very 'busy', that is, full of stage business (movements and gestures not directly indicated by the text) and with a lot of movement; very influenced by the work of Tyrone Guthrie, the director my generation most admired. We wanted our work to be like ballet, a form of theatre which we took very seriously. I had actors performing *ronds de jambes* as they spoke the rhyming couplets of Molière's *Le Misanthrope*. The costumes were camp abstract, and the audience as well as

71

the actors were in black and white. Later I came under the influence of Étienne Decroux, the Grand Old Man of Mime, the teacher of Jean-Louis Barrault and Marcel Marceau. One of Decroux's dicta was a quotation from Victor Hugo that nothing is more powerful than a statue that represents movement. My productions started to become more simple and more static. I stayed with Molière and did *George Dandin* in French, without set or period costumes, the actors sitting in a semicircle in full view of the audience, standing to mark their entrances and sitting for their exits. Even the different levels of the Dandin house were indicated by mime.

At this time everything stylish, elegant, seemed to come from Paris. In the search for a kind of purity, a true classicism, I went to Paris and watched the entire repertoire of the Comédie-Française, the simpler, more immediate productions of Jean Vilar at his Théâtre Nationale Populaire and the multi-stylish work of Barrault at the Marigny. This was 1952 and *Godot* was about to burst upon the world with its single tree designed by Giacometti. The idea of stillness and simplicity was already inherent in the French classical tradition. Barrault had his forays into total theatre but was constantly returning to the classical tradition—perhaps partly to please his wife, the wonderful Madeleine Renaud, whose training and whole career had been at the Comédie-Française. When Michael Redgrave and Peggy Ashcroft ran on the stage at the beginning of *Antony and Cleopatra* (RSC, 1953) at the Comédie-Française, the audience laughed. When the actors asked why they were told, 'In tragedy one never runs.' A fast entrance for Phèdre is unthinkable.

I was already disenchanted with French classicism when I first saw the work of Bertolt Brecht and his Berliner Ensemble in London in 1956, which altered my basic feelings and beliefs about theatre work. I had already seen *Mother Courage* at Vilar's theatre in Paris and Vilar's bare stage had some of the simple but aesthetically rich stage pictures of Brecht's work. Both used the focus of limited movement in the stage space. Vilar, being French, kept his actors still but their stillness never had the political intention of Brecht's own productions. Brecht was very influenced by his experience of oriental theatre: the controlled, detached technique of its actors, and the Noh theatre's extreme reduction of the principle of stillness in relation to action. I came to the plays of Zeami, the fourteenth-century dramatist, very late in my own work but I feel the underlying principles of the Noh theatre have always been there: a confirmation of the past and an opening to the future.

The American theatre artist Robert Wilson says that the two things not taught to actors in drama school are how to stand still and how to walk. His work is a reconsideration of movement on the stage and its effect. He will slow down a movement or an action to a point at which its nature is changed. This is not difficult to achieve but can become a cliché. Sometimes I set a group of actors an exercise in which they have to cross the width of the stage or the rehearsal room in exactly five minutes, monitoring their progress with a stopwatch. The walk, like the Noh walk, has to be even and regular, not speeded up or slowed down. The initial assessment of the space-time ratio is vital; the first step commits you to the overall pace. Some actors lose the sense of time to the extent that they take more than five minutes, some get there far too soon, and some have an uncanny sense of the right pace. They have to be alert but not involved. You mustn't dream and you mustn't panic. It is a form of meditation which is also an action. There is a movement from one point to another, a physical action which has taken place, but the lack of apparent dynamic, of the initial motivational impulse, and the absence of stress (in all its meanings—accent, anxiety) means it is not conventionally theatrical. It is opposed to the 'What do I need, what is my objective?' of the Stanislavsky school. It means that the action itself can be looked at by actor and audience in a detached manner, which is why the techniques of the oriental theatre suited Brecht's purpose.

At its simplest it is no more than the old trick of going into slow motion in moments of violence—a technique pioneered in film and since used very successfully in the theatre. (Apart from anything else, it stops the actors getting hurt.) Wilson has taken it to an extreme where it has become a mannerism and lost much of its value, but as a basis for an actor to be aware of his action and his identity as the performer, it is formidable. So much acting takes place at a tempo that is neither quick nor slow; a boring, inexpressive jog along, occasionally whipped up to create a false excitement. When in doubt keep still.

This is from a letter of John Gielgud's in 1976:

> The effect of rapid movement does greatly fascinate me both in the case of E.T. and H.I. [Ellen Terry and Henry Irving]. Have you noticed how Edith Evans never moves if she can help it? I never remember her entrances, and in Millamant's she was foiled by a stupid great gate, and had to enter through a narrow side archway. But she hardly ever moved in that part. She was like a Venetian glass figure in a vitrine, turning slowly now and then with slow deliberate movements of her neck and arms, never using her fan except as a kind of weapon! And whenever I have directed her— Bracknell, *Chalk Garden*, and the Nurse—she always wanted to stay still and let the voice do everything.

10
Sentences and Rhetoric—Wilde, Webster and Winston Churchill

In a speech, when you follow one sentence with another you make a structure. If the structure has an active function we call it rhetoric. Rhetoric was originally the art of persuasion through speaking—words used to influence people. It uses repetition with variation to make its effect. Think of Antony talking to the mob with his 'honourable men', which starts apparently sincerely but ends up in savage irony.

A sentence is a completed thought which is expressed as a unit (though, as I said earlier, not necessarily a unit of action). When you get to a full stop, something has been said, something has changed, something has moved forward. When speaking, you must not lose the thread of the development. That does not mean you cannot pause or interrupt the thought, but your audience must know that you haven't got to the end. The timing within the sentence is personal to the speaker.

Here are some sentences in a speech: Algernon in *The Importance of Being Earnest* is talking to his friend, Jack.

> I really don't see anything romantic in proposing. It is
> very romantic to be in love. But there is nothing
> romantic about a definite proposal. Why, one may be
> accepted. One usually is, I believe. Then the excitement
> is all over. The very essence of romance is uncertainty.
> If ever I get married, I'll certainly try to forget the fact.

Wilde creates the wit by the piling up of short, simple sentences, each complete in itself but with an expectation of comic development over the whole speech. The firmness of the full stops provides the audience with a moment in which they may laugh. When you read the passage you can see that there are various moments in which the audience might laugh—after 'accepted', after 'believe' and certainly after 'the fact'. The actor will only find this out with the audience and he may then have to decide to kill an early laugh in order to get a bigger one later. This requires skill and experience. It is as difficult to kill a laugh as get one.

Wilde's use of simple sentences without subordinate clauses is a kind of comic rhetoric. He is also the master of the long sentence. This is Lady Bracknell, from the same play:

> You can hardly imagine that I and Lord Bracknell
> would dream of allowing our only daughter—a girl
> brought up with the utmost care—to marry into a cloak
> room, and form an alliance with a parcel.

Here there is no question where the laugh comes.

The use of the compound sentence and subordinate clauses dwindled in the twentieth century. Sentences became generally shorter. The dash, the parenthesis were less frequent and started to be replaced by enigmatic rows of dots, which mean different things to each individual writer. This is Foster, one of Hirst's servants/hitmen in Pinter's *No Man's Land*, talking about how he came to be employed:

> I was in Bali when they sent for me. I didn't have to
> leave, I didn't have to come here. But I felt I was…
> called… I had no alternative. I didn't have to leave that
> beautiful isle. But I was intrigued. I was only a boy. But
> I was nondescript and anonymous. A famous writer
> wanted me. He wanted me to be his secretary, his
> chauffeur, his housekeeper, his amanuensis. How did he
> know of me? Who told him?

Pinter does not build a climax in the speech, there is no crescendo. The speech is over when the character stops speaking. It has, if anything, increased our area of unknowing but it is a kind of rhetoric.

Edward Bond uses short sentences but he has a more catholic use of phrasing and sometimes will use accumulated phrases to make a sour rhetoric. This is from *Early Morning*, an allegorical fantasy of the court of Queen Victoria. Gladstone is seen as a ruthless and vicious trades union leader in charge of couple of thugs. He strolls round the stage as the thugs beat up a young Cockney lad, saying:

> Time! Time! Suddenly the birds come, it's spring,
> suddenly they mate, suddenly they 'atch, the young fly, a
> few days and they're gone, the sickle's already in the
> corn, the fruit falls, the old man leans on 'is 'oe,
> suddenly 'e looks up, it's winter, and the skull's already
> on the window-sill.

which is certainly rhetorical but surely ironic in the context of the scene.

Much contemporary writing consists of simplifying the structure of rhetoric, while making it more ambiguous. Rhetoric for the Renaissance writer was so full of emotion it could express itself as powerfully in one line as over a long speech. My old tutor, F.W. Bateson, wrote this:

> With Renaissance literature, whether it is prose or
> verse, the words have all the immediacy and
> resonance of splendid speech—a speech that itself
> controls and determines the nature of the dramatic
> action. The literary unit, therefore, is a speech unit, a
> phrase or a single sentence, as is clearly demonstrated
> by the large number of memorable items bequeathed
> by English Renaissance literature to any dictionary of
> quotations.
>
> (F.W. Bateson, *A Guide to English Literature*)

He gives the example of Duke Ferdinand's famous line from Webster's *The Duchess of Malfi*—

> Cover her face; mine eyes dazzle; she died young...

which he says is like a miniature three-act play. In the play Ferdinand has tortured—and finally ordered the death of—his sister. He has vowed not to look upon her while she lives. Now she is dead he looks at her and then tells Bosola to cover her face. The sentence is made up of three phrases: the first an order, the second a description of his reaction to the sight of the dead body, the third a comment. The impact of the line depends on the separate identity of each phrase and the imaginative unity of the three phrases together. Only at the end of the line do we have the full experience, even if we are not sure what it means. Does it express Ferdinand's remorse? That feels too simple an explanation and the line would be ruined if the actor tried to inject such a feeling into it. He has to give each part of the line equal value and let it speak for itself. The line has a magic even when one does not know the context, but the context at once limits and opens its potential meaning. Sometimes lines resonate regardless of their context. I can't now remember either the speaker or the context of the line in Marlowe's *The Jew of Malta*:

> But that was in another country,
> And besides, the wench is dead.

And now it would spoil my appreciation of the line to find out. The line from Webster is a complex juxtaposition of simple phrases in an unusual order. How much more straightforward it would be if it read:

> Mine eyes dazzle; she died young; cover her face.

Or:

> She died young; mine eyes dazzle; cover her face.

It would also solve the problem of when exactly Bosola is to cover the face. But Webster wrote:

Cover her face; mine eyes dazzle; she died young.

The phrase order suggests the uncertainty and complexity of Ferdinand's feelings. The need for the face to be covered comes first. Is he still looking at the face or does he turn away after the order? The preceding dialogue is:

BOSOLA. Fix your eyes here.

FERDINAND. Constantly.

The 'constantly' suggests a fixed stare, difficult to break from. 'Mine eyes dazzle' suggests 1) tears, 2) reaction to her beauty. 'She died young' is the most puzzling. Regret that she has died too soon and it's his fault? It is the supreme example of a line which has its own life and must not be coloured by the actor.

Sometimes a speech in a play may not be rhetorical in the sense of an outgoing action, but is composed in a form which has a kind of internal rhetoric. In Hamlet's 'O, that this too, too solid flesh would melt' soliloquy the development of the central line of thought is tortuous.

> That it should come to this—
> But two months dead—nay, not so much, not two—
> So excellent a king, that was to this
> Hyperion to a satyr, so loving to my mother
> That he might not beteem the winds of heaven
> Visit her face too roughly! Heaven and earth,
> Must I remember? Why, she would hang on him
> As if increase of appetite had grown
> By what it fed on, and yet within a month—
> Let me not think on't; frailty thy name is woman—
> A little month, or ere those shoes were old
> With which she followed my poor father's body,
> Like Niobe, all tears, why she, even she—
> O, God, a beast that wants discourse of reason
> Would have mourned longer!—married with mine
>   uncle,
> My father's brother, but no more like my father

> Than I to Hercules; within a month,
> Ere yet the salt of most unrighteous tears
> Had left the flushing of her gallèd eyes,
> She married.

The repetition of 'month' holds the speech together. To begin with we are unclear as to who is the subject of the action. Is it the father or the mother? But by the time we get to 'why she, even she' we are in no doubt. There is a simple sentence running through the speech which struggles for expression:

> But two months dead—nay, not so much, not two
> ………….. and yet within a month
> A little month…………………………………………
> …………………………………….she, even she
> …………………………….married with mine uncle
> …………………………………….within a month
> She married.

We have been taken on a journey with the character in which he has forced himself to relive what hurts him to remember, but the dreadful fact has to be spoken.

When Churchill was preparing his wartime speeches he would set them out on the page like poetry, with the phrasing with which he would deliver them. This is an example from his notes:

> We shall fight on the beaches,
>   we shall fight on the landing grounds,
>   we shall fight in the fields and in the streets,
>   we shall fight in the hills;
> we shall never surrender.

He was using the means of the actor: employing a literary form to have an emotional—in his case a political—effect. As he prepared the speech he was already hearing how it would sound when spoken. He sets his text out for that purpose:

Not only great dangers,
  but many more misfortunes,
    many shortcomings,
      many mistakes,
        many disappointments
will surely be our lot.

Death and sorrow will be the companions
  of our journey,
    hardship our garment:
constancy and valour are our
  only shield.

We must be united:
  we must be undaunted.

Now it exists as a piece of history, a passage of literature; then it was an immediate response to a critical situation. The success of its rhetoric depends on the listener being aware of the speaker's purpose, that the phrases are building to a resolution. Something is expected of us. The literary form is experienced as waves of energy, which is how we received it in 1940. When we heard Tony Blair in the House of Commons persuading us of the necessity of the war with Iraq, we knew that his rhetorical phrases had no development. They were accompanied by the two hands pushing the lies into us, with that peculiar, downward, chopping motion which is typical of politicians today. He was not in an historic moment to which we had to respond; he was creating a false one.

An actor has to expand or contract his energy span with the writing. In the process he will start to feel the style of the period, the writer and perhaps the character, but most of all the movement of the action. Each phrase has its own life and must be experienced:

We shall fight on the beaches...

But it is the conclusion of the sentence:

we shall never surrender.

81

which completes the thought and moves the action forward. At the full stop we grit our teeth in 1940 or charge into the breach at Harfleur or rush out to kill the murderers of Caesar. In each case a master rhetorician—Churchill, Henry V, Mark Antony—has worked upon us.

Churchill was a man steeped in literature who could quote huge passages of *Paradise Lost* from memory and constantly modelled his rhetoric on the Bible:

> The earth is the Lord's, and the fullness thereof;
> the world, and they that dwell therein.
>
> For he hath founded it upon the seas,
> and established it upon the floods.

> (Psalm 24)

The Psalm is not active. It doesn't incite or lead to an action, like Churchill's speech. It expresses a spacious certainty which comes from the formal repetition of the same ideas in different words. It is incantatory not dynamic. But its rhythmic weight is the same. Political rhetoric depends on the massing of idea on idea until there is no escape.

Sometimes the rhetoric is just one sentence, as in John of Gaunt's famous speech about England in *Richard II*, Act 2, Scene 1. Gaunt is old and dying and is visited by the King. Gaunt says he is 'a prophet new inspired' and has a vision of the state of the nation. We don't know what form this prophecy will take. The sentence, which lasts twenty lines, begins 'This royal throne of kings, this sceptred isle…' During the Second World War it was used as a paean of nationalism, an encouragement to patriotism; it was even set to music. To achieve this it had to be discreetly edited so that it became a list of subjects without a main verb. In the play when the verb arrives it is devastating and alters the meaning of everything that precedes it. The list of subjects, all in apposition, is like this:

> This royal throne of kings,
> this sceptred isle,
> This earth of majesty,
> this seat of Mars,
> This other Eden...
> This fortress...
> This happy breed...
> this little world,
> This precious stone...
> This blessed plot,
> this earth,
> this realm,
> this England,
> this nurse,
> this teeming womb of royal kings...
> This land of such dear souls,
> this dear, dear land

and then the verb arrives (I have cut out the subordinate clauses which make it even more dense):

> IS NOW LEASED OUT—I die pronouncing it—
> Like to a tenement or pelting farm.

One more sentence recapitulates the whole idea, ending with:

> That England that was wont to conquer others
> Hath made a shameful conquest of itself.

Hardly a sentiment for wartime. The rhetorical device is excessive but effective if the actor can sustain it with variety and power. The richness of each individual phrase must not clog the movement of the sentence. The extended list of subjects is shattered by the brutality of the verb 'is now leased out', which is intensified by the parenthesis of 'I die pronouncing it'. That does not mean that Gaunt's despair must be anticipated. The knowledge of where the sentence is going will colour the actor's feeling but it must not become clear until we hit the verb.

In 'What a piece of work is a man', Hamlet's disillusion gives an overall key to the speech, but the extent of his bitterness must not be apparent until:

> And yet, to me, what is this quintessence of dust? Man delights not me…

We must be seduced by the words with which Hamlet describes the wonder of man before we encounter his bitterness. When Nicol Williamson played it, he snarled his way all through the speech. There was no doubt from the beginning of Hamlet's misanthropy and no surprise at the development of his thought. The phrases must be sweet while they are sweet, and become sour with the feeling. All musicians are aware of this as one of the basic elements of their work. They live within the smaller phrase without losing the overall direction of the music. For the actor it's the phrase in the sentence, the sentence in the speech, the speech in the action of the play. But an actor, even an actor playing Hamlet, is only responsible for the dynamic movement of his own part. He has to know where his character is going, but the play itself has its own momentum.

The movement of a sentence is the same in verse or prose. The sense of a line moves towards the full stop even if it is in the middle of a blank verse line. (I totally disagree with Peter Hall who thinks you should stop at the end of every line of blank verse and never pause in the middle of a line.) Shakespeare spent his working life exploring the flexibility of the iambic pentameter. As he matured he not only the dropped the use of rhyme but 'end-stopping', in which the thought is completed at the end of the line and a pause is natural, becomes less frequent. The sense spills over from line to line, the syntax becomes more fluid, more expressive. The sentence moves against the pattern of the verse; moves, not nearer to prose, but to a greater poetic complexity.

In *The Winter's Tale*, Leontes is with his son, Mamillius, and watches his wife, Hermione, and his friend, Polixenes, leaving the stage. He mistakenly believes they are lovers and he tells us what he feels. The speech has moments in which he talks to the boy, who is too young to know the meaning of the rest of the speech.

> Gone already.
> Inch thick, knee deep, o'er head and ears a forked one!
> Go play, boy, play Thy mother plays, and I
> Play too, but so disgraced a part, whose issue
> Will hiss me to my grave. Contempt and clamour
> Will be my knell. Go play, boy, play. There have been,
> Or I am much deceived, cuckolds ere now,
> And many a man there is, even at this present,
> Now while I speak this, holds his wife by th'arm.
> That little thinks she has been sluiced in's absence,
> And his pond fished by his next neighbour, by
> Sir Smile, his neighbour.
>
> (*The Winter's Tale* 1.2)

The second line is a sentence without a verb or an object and a very cryptic subject. It is the spilling-out of passion and unleashes the rest of the speech. No actor would pause after 'I' in line three, or 'issue' in line four and certainly not after 'by' in line eleven. The actor must go with the sentences. The irregular rhythm and structure exactly convey the turmoil that Leontes is in. Keeping the boy on the stage and making him part of the soliloquy is pure genius. The way the sentences break the verse, and the short phrases and repetitions break the sentences, are the actor's musical markings. The blank verse norm is necessary for the breaking of it to be expressive.

Sentences in plays used to be longer than they are now. Probably sentences in life were longer than they are now. The increased speed of travel and communication has led to the sound bite and the clipped phrase. The attention span necessary to hold on to the thought of a long sentence has diminished. The First World War marked the death of the long sentence, or at least its decline. The elaborate sentences of Proust are part of a nostalgia for a world that no longer exists. In dramatic writing the world of Oscar Wilde is one of summer afternoons, cucumber sandwiches and arching phrases. It was not to last for him after his trial in 1895, or for anyone else after 1914. Most of George Bernard Shaw's best plays were written before the First World War, and, though he continued to write with assured rhetorical flourish, he was increasingly out of step. The short, clipped sentences of Noël Coward, the most successful writer of the inter-war years, marked a huge change in playwriting and consequently in actors' speaking. From the point of view of style, there is a much bigger gap between Wilde and Coward than there is between Coward and Pinter.

11
Phrasing and Pauses—Congreve and Beckett

When I listen to actors reading I don't look at the text but try to understand what is being said, as if I were hearing it for the first time. Occasionally I stop and say, 'Is that a full stop or a comma? I can't tell.' I don't mean, 'Have you observed the punctuation?' but rather, 'I can't hear whether your thought has got anywhere. Is it complete?' Too often a sentence is left hanging in mid-air. For me the only punctuation invariably to be marked by a pause is the full stop. Commas, colons, semicolons, are aids to understanding, and sometimes breathing, but only the full stop shows whether the actor has understood the progression of the writing. In that sense the believers in 'actioning' are right. If the actor is not living in the moment and is already thinking of his next sentence he will not finish the thought of the one he is in. He does not commit himself to the line as part of the development of the play. A text is built up of phrases, of which the most defined is the sentence, and the phrases may need pauses either for breath or clarification. It is the actor's business to find them and to build his performance from them. A play is like a score, but, unlike music, it translates not only into sound, but into the action of which sound is a part. And it is not the sound of the words but their meaning which makes it part of the action. The audiences of today may have less response to words than previous generations, but actors must still learn the relationship between text and action, between the shape of the words on the page and their performance on stage.

Punctuation varies from writer to writer and from century to century. Here is some of Hamlet's first soliloquy as it appears in the First Folio:

> That it should come to this:
> But two months dead: Nay, not so much; not two,
> So excellent a King, that was to this
> *Hiperion* to a Satyre: so loving to my Mother,
> That he might not beteene the windes of heaven
> Visit her face too roughly. Heaven and Earth
> Must I remember: why she would hang on him,
> As if encrease of Appetite had growne
> By what it fed on; and yet within a month?
> Let me not thinke on't: Frailty thy name is woman.

How does it differ from the Oxford editors' version (see page 79)? There are no dashes before 'not so much'; this and the other interjections are marked by colons. There are the capital letters on certain key nouns. There is no question mark after 'must I remember' and a rather odd one after 'within a month'. It looks more staid than the modern edition. Does it make much difference for the actor? The exclamations still interrupt the flow of the speech, there are still the insistent repetitions of 'within a month' intensifying but holding up the articulation of the main clause. The character of the speech is the same and will be found by the actor whatever the punctuation.

Dashes are rare in Shakespeare (no doubt the purists frowned upon them as they do today), but they are a very convenient shorthand to convey instability. Sometimes an entire comic character can be built on the dash. This is Jingle in *The Pickwick Papers*, talking about a cricket match in India:

> Warm!—red hot—scorching—glowing. Played a match
> once—single wicket—friend the Colonel—Sir Thomas
> Blazo—who should get the greatest number of runs.—

Won the toss—first innings—seven o'clock A.M.—six
natives to look out—went in; kept in—heat intense—
natives all fainted—taken away—fresh half-dozen
ordered—fainted also—Blazo bowling—supported by
two natives—couldn't bowl me out—fainted too—
cleared away the Colonel—wouldn't give in—faithful
attendant—Quanko Samba—last man left—sun so hot,
bat in blisters, ball scorched brown—five hundred and
seventy runs—rather exhausted—Quanko mustered up
last remaining strength—bowled me out—had a bath,
and went out to dinner.

This is great fun but it can have no dramatic development.
The character doesn't change with changing situations. It is
as fixed as a comedian's catchphrases. In Congreve's *The
Way of the World* the dash is used more subtly. This is the
ageing Lady Wishfort, preparing to receive her supposed
admirer, Sir Rowland, talking to her maid, Foible:

But art thou sure Sir Rowland will not fail to come? Or
will a' not fail when he does come? Will he be
importunate, Foible, and push? For if he should not be
importunate—I shall never break decorums—I shall
die with confusion, if I am forced to advance—Oh no,
I can never advance—I shall swoon if he should expect
advances—No, I hope Sir Rowland is better bred than
to put a lady to the necessity of breaking her forms. I
won't be too coy neither—I won't give him despair—
but a little disdain is not amiss—a little scorn is alluring.

Notice how the repetition of words holds the speech
together through the character's comic uncertainty and
excitement, expressed by the dashes. Foible, the maid, reas-
sures her, and the dashes disappear.

FOIBLE. By storm, madam. Sir Rowland's a brisk man.

LADY WISHFORT. Is he? Oh, then he'll importune, if he's
a brisk man. I shall save decorums if Sir Rowland
importunes. I have a mortal terror at the
apprehension of offending against decorums.

Nothing but importunity can surmount decorums.
Oh, I'm glad he's a brisk man.

The very word 'brisk' has calmed the punctuation down but the repetition of words carries on.

In the same play the admired, but impossible Mrs Millamant is explaining why she is late. She turns to her maid:

MILLAMANT. Ay, that's true. Oh, but then I had—
Mincing, what had I? Why was I so long?

MINCING. Oh, mem, your la'ship stayed to peruse a pecket of letters.

MILLAMANT. Oh, ay, letters! I had letters. I am persecuted with letters—I hate letters—Nobody knows how to write letters, and yet one has 'em, one does not know why—They serve one to pin up one's hair.

The short sentences, the repetitions, provide the rhythm of the character or the comic rhythm of the scene, as far as they can be separated. All the actor needs to do is to observe the musical markings. Comic rhetoric, unlike the political rhetoric we looked at in the last chapter, does not advance by inexorable repetitions to a climax, like Antony's with his 'honourable men'. Instead, the repetitions hover round the situation and sometimes come to rest, like a butterfly.

When I directed the play in 1984 Maggie Smith played Millamant. She was as brilliant as Edith Evans, who famously played it sixty years earlier, and who, to judge from the recordings, was completely different. Evans had a kind of serene mockery, Smith a nervous high spirits. I took issue with Maggie over her phrasing of the following:

Beauty the lover's gift! Lord, what is a lover that it can give? Why, one makes lovers as fast as one pleases, and they live as long as one pleases, and they die as soon as one pleases; and then, if one pleases one makes more.

Maggie would stress only one pair of antithetical words—'and they **live** as long as one pleases and they **die** as soon as one pleases...'—when to get the balance right (and to the Augustan mind balance was everything) you have to stress both pairs of contrasting words—'they **live** as **long** as one pleases, and they **die** as **soon** as one pleases; and **then**...' A succession of pairs of contrasting words is typical of the Restoration period. Antithesis is not quite the right word because the compared words may be parallel rather than opposed. In speaking, the compared word should be marked by variations of pitch rather than weight. The repetition of 'pleases' keeps the idea on the ground, stops the writing taking off either into poetry or passion. Antithesis had been used by Shakespeare, but the use of it to express the desired balance of society reached its fulfilment in the eighteenth century. Milton wrote two poems on contrasting themes, *L'Allegro* and *Il Penseroso*. When Handel set them to music a third alternative had to be found, a middle way: *Il Moderato*. Reason had to find the balance. Sometimes the search for a balance through the tightly controlled sentence becomes pompous. Earlier in Congreve's play Millamant's lover Mirabell says to her:

> I say that a man may as soon make a friend by his wit,
> or a fortune by his honesty, as win a woman with plain
> dealing and sincerity.

On one hand 'friend', 'fortune', 'woman', on the other 'wit', 'honesty', and 'plain dealing and sincerity'. Doesn't it sound rather smug? Millamant rightly replies, 'Sententious Mirabell'—and his is a rather thankless part. Millamant and Lady Wishfort are the more vivid characters and the ones that appeal most to the audience. (No actor ever made his name playing Mirabell.) This is partly because Congreve created Millamant and Wishfort with some of the exuberance, almost Jonsonian, of an earlier period.

This use of the balanced phrase persisted through the nineteenth century. Wilde's Lady Bracknell uses it all the time:

> What between the duties **expected** of one during one's
> **lifetime** and the duties **exacted** from one after one's
> **death**, land has ceased to be either a **profit** or a
> **pleasure**. It **gives** one **position**, and **prevents** one from
> **keeping it up**. That's all that can be said about land.

Again the repetition of 'duties' ballasts the sentence and
highlights the antithetical words. And the long sentence is
followed by the short to create the anticlimax and the laugh.
It is mock rhetoric. It also conveys a character entirely sure
of herself. By her broken phrases Millamant might seem
unsure of herself—but, in fact, her stops and starts are part
of her armoury.

Peter Gill, who is both writer and director, has an interesting exercise for actors. He gives an actor a passage of text
completely unpunctuated. After study the actor has to speak
the speech to the rest of the group to make the sense as he
or she understands it. The group may question the clarity
of the delivery and the actor has to rethink it until the audi-
tors fully understand the passage. This is a much better way
than working from the punctuation. Gill's exercise concen-
trates on communication through speaking. The small
pauses that an actor makes are personal to him or her, but
provided the sense is clear and the speech keeps moving
there are no fixed rules.

The last chapter of James Joyce's *Ulysses* (written between
1914 and 1921) is a completely unpunctuated monologue
spoken by Molly Bloom:

> Yes because he never did a thing like that before as ask
> to get his breakfast in bed with a couple of eggs since
> the City Arms hotel when he used to be pretending to
> be laid up with a sick voice doing his highness to make
> himself interesting to that old faggot Mrs Riordan that
> he thought he had a great leg of and she never left us a
> farthing all for masses for herself and her soul greatest
> miser ever was actually afraid to lay out 4d for her
> methylated spirit...

And so she goes on for thirty-six pages. It is interesting that, in spite of the absence of punctuation, the sense is rarely in doubt. It is no more difficult than the rest of the novel. If you read it aloud you automatically add commas to make it clearer. It is the supreme example of what is called 'stream of consciousness'. It represents the unbroken, life-affirming, female principle as opposed to the rational, ordered, punctuated death of the male sentence.

Death, damnation and hellfire are the underlying themes of Lucky's unpunctuated monologue in *Waiting for Godot*:

> ...but time will tell I resume alas alas on on in short in
> fine on on abode of stones who can doubt it I resume
> but not so fast I resume the skull fading fading fading
> and concurrently simultaneously what is more for
> reasons unknown in spite of the tennis on on the beard
> the flames the tears the stones so blue so calm alas alas
> on on the skull the skull the skull the skull in
> Connemara...

This is not unlike some of Beckett's poems where the repetition of words or phrases with variations represents a search for the words that will unlock the meaning of life, or death. A search which, by its nature, can never be fulfilled.

In Beckett's *Play* each character speaks in neat phrases a narrative of his or her own, written in the clichés of a pulp magazine. Note, no dashes. Short sentences with full stops.

> w2. She came again. Just strolled in. All honey. Licking
> her lips. Poor thing. I was doing my nails, by the open
> window. He has told me all about it, she said. Who
> he, I said, filing away, and what it? I know what
> torture you must be going through, she said, and I
> have dropped in to say I bear you no ill-feeling. I rang
> for Erskine.

It's almost Noël Coward. But it is spoken by a decaying body in an urn; the narrative is continually interrupted by the stories of the other two corpses and it is spoken very fast in a monotone, without expression, in short, stabbing phrases. The speed of the delivery was dictated by Beckett as director but the phrasing is in the text. It is not quite Dalek speech, in which there is an equal pause between one syllable and the next, or the automated phone voice Directory Enquiries which gives you a number where each digit has been recorded separately and at a different pitch.

An actor can learn the musical form of what he says even before he knows why he is saying it. But it is more common for an actor to make decisions about the emotion of a speech before he has fully explored its formal and rhythmic structure. This denies the text its full expressiveness. Conversely there are actors who intuitively hear the music of the writing and can make sense of something they do not fully understand. An actor must feel the shape of the phrase or the sentence and try to inhabit it. It is impossible to do this without some basic awareness of character and situation and the direction of the scene, but it is equally impossible to act without the ability to feel the phrasing. Though the punctuation may be in doubt, the actor must still search for the right phrasing, the dramatic music. The structural make-up of a sentence can be analysed by reading, but the true process is by the ear or, more precisely, by the eye, the ear and the tongue.

Pauses

Two comedians are discussing how to interest an audience:

> FIRST COMEDIAN. If they don't want to amuse themselves they can make do with silence.
>
> SECOND COMEDIAN. They'll never stand for it.
>
> FIRST COMEDIAN. We can break it up with dialogue from time to time if it would make you any easier. And silence isn't so easy to come by as all that, either, if it comes to that.

SECOND COMEDIAN. It's not what you go to a theatre for.
  You go to other places for silence. Not a theatre.
  They'll feel cheated.

(N.F. Simpson, *A Resounding Tinkle*)

In Shakespeare's day they would certainly have felt cheated.
There is only one marked pause in the whole of
Shakespeare. In *Coriolanus*, after Volumnia's long speech to
her son, pleading with him to spare Rome, the stage
direction is:

He holds her hand, silent.

before Coriolanus says:

O, mother, mother!
  What have you done?

(*Coriolanus* 5.3)

How did the Elizabethans manage without pauses and, more
pertinently, why do we need them now? Plays by aspiring
writers today are peppered with the meaningless direction
'*Beat*'. For an Elizabethan writer one speech followed
another without pause, and the text must have been spoken
quickly or 'the two hours' traffic of our stage' is nonsense.
The emotion of the characters was never hidden, except
where it was kept for soliloquy. It pours out in the richest
imagery. The play does not need pauses because the character listening absorbs the emotional content of the speaker's
words as they are spoken, and so is ready to respond immediately. This is conveyed by a shift in key between the two
voices. No musician would have difficulty understanding
this, but actors of today feel they need time to react before
they reply. They make an intellectual rather than a musical
response. It is only in the twentieth century that the writer
chose to write pauses as part of the printed text.

How did this come about? There was the move towards
naturalism at the end of the nineteenth century with the
plays of Chekhov and the new approach of the Moscow

Art Theatre. There was the arrival of the cinema where the visual demands parity with, and finally supremacy over, the spoken word. The power and the poetry of the imagined image was replaced by that of the visible picture. Listen to the soundtrack of most films with your eyes shut and you soon realise how few words there are and how little potency they have without the picture. The image of an actor in close-up, responding to a situation, replaces the need for words. (I said earlier that the remembered great moments of the old theatre were ones of reacting, and so they were; but they were at key moments and there were few of them and often in indifferent plays.) This still does not explain why dramatists should have started to use pauses. For a long time they resisted. There are no pauses to speak of in Shaw. But there are a plethora of stage directions, including adverbs to describe the character's tone, which actors dislike because it pre-empts their interpretation of the part. With Shaw they are mainly decorative, but for other writers the stage directions start to have a temporal life and affect the rhythm of the playing. This is combined with the shortening of sentences.

With *Waiting for Godot* the whole framework changes. I think of it as the original play of pauses, and so it probably is, but when I look at the first few pages of the play I find few pauses, but an enormous number of stage directions—both adverbs dictating the emotional tone of the playing, and elaborate descriptions of physical business, which are as much part of the play as the spoken words. The business is precisely described and is surely meant to happen separately from the words. This, more than anything, alters the rhythm of the play. Instead of business being an addition to the text, it is part of it, and so, when they happen, are the pauses.

> VLADIMIR. There's a man all over for you, blaming on his boots the faults of his feet. (*He takes off his hat again, looks inside it, feels about inside it, knocks on the*

crown, blows into it, puts it on again.) This is getting alarming. (*Silence. Vladimir deep in thought, Estragon pulling at his toes.*) One of the thieves was saved. (*Pause.*) It's a reasonable percentage. (*Pause.*) Gogo.

ESTRAGON. What?

VLADIMIR. Suppose we repented.

ESTRAGON. Repented what?

VLADIMIR. Oh... (*He reflects.*) We wouldn't have to go into the details.

ESTRAGON. Our being born?

I think a Renaissance writer saw life as full of opportunity and as a continuous excitement. Every moment was full and there was no time to pause; even meditation was voiced. For Shakespeare, time was the enemy to be fought. For Beckett, time had ceased to exist, except as a void to be filled momentarily by phrases of philosophy, religion or trivial gossip. The talk of the two tramps in *Godot* resembles the patter of comedians. But true comedians make their own timing which is tested by the audience's response—or lack of it. Beckett actually writes pauses into the text. Sometimes the lines get laughs, sometimes they don't. The life of the play does not depend on them. The silences are part of the play's structure.

There are no tips to be given to actors about timing. Beckett and Pinter, by their exact instructions, wanted a greater control of the actor. Pinter insisted on the difference between five and six dots, and between '*Pause*' and '*Silence*'; Beckett debated the number of steps in *Footfall*, and actors, being by nature willing, have gone along with them. But in performance an actor will always vary his timing infinitesimally. It is the intuitive awareness of exactly how long to pause that gets the biggest laugh. Ralph Lynn, the great farceur of the 1920s, used to whisper under his breath to the younger actors he was working with, 'Don't say it yet, don't say it yet. Say it... now,' and he was always right.

Beckett wants to change the audience's perception by altering the received idea of theatre time. Sometimes everything is unbearably slow, like Clov's ritual of looking through the windows and moving the stepladder in the opening of *Endgame*, sometimes everything hurtles along like the three damned souls in their urns in *Play*. But all the characters are equally imprisoned.

> CLOV. What is there to keep me here?
>
> HAMM. The dialogue.

> *(Endgame)*

12
Masks and Action—Ben Jonson

The Gower Street entrance to the Royal Academy of Dramatic Art is flanked by the figures of Comedy and Tragedy wearing their masks. The masks look as if they are huge concrete crash helmets that the figures are trying to prise off, rather like Michelangelo's unfinished *Slaves* in the Accademia in Florence. The two masks are the abiding symbol of the actor's art, but, in spite of the reverent persistence of Peter Hall, the very word 'mask' fills most theatre practitioners with dread or contempt, as does the phrase *Commedia dell'Arte*. Peter Brook doesn't use masks.

I was excited by acting in masks, which was taught me by my master, George Devine, the first director of the Royal Court, who had it from his mentor Michel Saint-Denis, who had it from Jacques Copeau. Saint-Denis always differentiated between, on the one hand, the Comic or Character mask as used in the Italian comedy, a half-mask with the chin and mouth revealed, and, on the other, the Classic mask, a full mask with a closed mouthpiece and used in short, serious scenarios, which has some affinities with the Neutral mask used in mime. Neither has anything to do with the Japanese Noh mask, of which I have little experience; I only worked in the comic mask.

The way of working is strikingly simple. Various masks are laid out on a table, with a medium-sized mirror so that you can see yourself from the waist upward, without bending. There are also hats, sticks and small accessories available. You put on the mask, look in the mirror and see a completely new being. You respond immediately to what you see, leave the mirror, maybe choose a hat to complete the new personality and possibly a simple prop like a stick. In the moment you are transformed, or should be, and become the new person. With a successful assumption the character of the mask is seen to take over your body, from the neck through the shoulders to the feet. It is always clear when this is done truthfully. If you consciously try to create the kind of movement you think the mask ought to do, it is immediately seen to be false. Your mind wishes to remain in control. Those watching can see the actor under the mask and not the new being you should have become. You have to believe that you have been taken over. The assumption of the new persona doesn't last long and you must not keep the mask on if you feel the character slipping. Later you repeat the exercise in pairs and eventually the masks learn to speak—a difficult process. For brief moments you will see theatre at its most intense and basic. You feel as if you are tapping into the religious roots of drama. And perhaps you are. The only thing is that it doesn't last and it is difficult to shape the work into the requirements of a play, written or otherwise.

I made various attempts to marry the mask to written texts—in John Arden's *The Happy Haven* (Royal Court, 1960), a Jonsonian comedy written to be performed in masks, and in *The Caucasian Chalk Circle* (RSC, 1962), where their use had been sanctioned by Brecht—but it never worked. The characters created by the masks resented having to speak lines not their own. They are wilful, selfish creatures governed by obsessive needs and feel no responsibility to the writer and the narrative. Above all they are not interested in the movement of the play. The acting process demands a transition from the intuitive beginning to the conscious application of skill. (*Commedia dell'Arte* means 'comedy of skill' and the nearest translation of the Japanese word *Noh* is 'skill'). Even when successful, a mask will lead to clowning or stand-up comedy rather than a written character. It will create the comedian's persona. You can actually see Chaplin at work at it in his early films, searching for the physical statement of his comic persona, till he finds the hat, the stick, the boots that make up the tramp image we all know. Olivier hated the whole idea of masks but his use of externals was the starting point of his work—straight nose for Oedipus, eyebrows and blacked-out tooth as Archie Rice, buck teeth for Shylock—and constituted a kind of mask acting. But the whole idea of acting as transformation through externals has almost disappeared. Look at the photographs of Stanislavsky in all the parts he played; look at Ralph Richardson's drawings of his make-up as Caliban; think of a young actor being *allowed* to play Fagin now as Guinness was in the 1948 film of *Oliver Twist*. Or Orson Welles as the ageing Kane.

I made one attempt to create a play which would satisfy the masks by letting them improvise in performance. This was *An Optimistic Thrust* (Joint Stock, 1979), created entirely by the actors, without a writer. The rehearsals sometimes seemed like a dream world in which strange creations from literature and the actors' imagination would meet in improvisation. We had sessions in which we created our own 'ghosts', the personification of those influences on our lives that still haunted us. Predictably, most people created versions of their parents, usually fathers for the men and mothers for the women, and the work moved close to a kind of drama therapy, though anarchy and humour would break through. But in the end we started to feel the lack of a writer to shape the material and we had to structure the show ourselves. We had faithfully taped our improvisations and transcribed them, but on the page they seemed dead. In performance it was impossible to keep the spontaneity of the original moment. But it was an exciting period of work.

It is impossible to be totally improvisatory every night. Many comedians approach their work as if they were going to improvise and perhaps vary their material in some details, which will refire their creativity or even recycle material from previous performances. They feel free. What we call timing is this ability to vary the time element sufficiently for the actor to feel as if it is new and for the audience to share this sensation.

I have an exercise for actors, not in masks, which is very like mask work. You are asked to describe someone you know in the third person and, as you describe them, to become the character, imitating the externals of voice, movement, etc. (It's better if the person is not known to the rest of the group.) You then have to speak a speech or poem, which you already know by heart but which is completely uncon- nected to the character you have created. The imagination works intuitively to connect the two. (Guaranteed to create gales of mirth!) It is a good exercise and demonstrates to the actor that he, not the writer, can be in charge of the play. But it is basically an extension of impersonation, a training for Rory Bremners rather than actors. Everything is pre- sented from the outside. There is no identification with the inner life of the character or the movement of the scene. In fact there is no scene to move. Stanislavsky would stress an identification with the character and his needs as pre- ceding the externals of voice and movement, but in his later years he thought that the essence of acting was to find the right physical action and to be able to justify it.

The analogy with music is tempting but can be misleading. The musician is detached from his instrument: he picks it up and plays the music in the rhythm and tempo in which it is written. He cannot impose his timing (unless he is playing the cadenza in a concerto). It has to be worked and lived through. Drama is not like that, though sometimes I wish it were. The actor is his own instrument. He not only has to play the written score of the text, he has to embody a character who does not exist, and that must to some extent mean creating his own timing. A play has to be seen as well as heard. The actor must feel the phrasing and make observance of the markings of pace and rhythm as his own. I believe this is ultimately true even in the strictest productions of Brecht or Beckett. Very few plays are as finely structured as a Mozart symphony; most productions of Shakespeare will have some cuts and there are alternative versions of the text. The theatre has never been a pure art.

Jonson and Shakespeare

The mask is the symbol of the actor's work, his assumption of character. Aristotle thought character was not the most important element in drama, being always subservient to action. Comic, masked characters are obsessive and static, and can only express their needs: greed, lust, self-importance are common examples. They resent action unless it fulfils their needs and have to be moved by the narrative rather than motivate it. The 'humour' characters in Jonson are the written equivalent of mask acting. In *The Alchemist* the characters are either manipulators or their dupes. They all need money to satisfy their desires. Sir Epicure Mammon, in a wonderful speech, tells us what he will do with the money:

> Then my glasses,
> Cut in more subtle angles, to disperse
> And multiply the figures as I walk
> Naked between my *succubae*. My mists
> I'll have of perfume, vapoured 'bout the room
> To lose ourselves in; and my baths, like pits
> To fall into: from whence we will come forth,
> And roll us dry in gossamer and roses.
>
> (*The Alchemist* 2.2)

The picture becomes richer and more extravagant as it goes on, a dream of the refinement of the senses, but at the end of the speech we are no further forward in the action. Nothing has changed. Mammon is left with his dreams and never realises them. The speech is a piece of comic rhetoric, built on a list of sensual images. It depends on the virtuosity of the actor to carry it. But it does create a 'nowness' of physical sensation. Jonson's poem 'Her Triumph' does the same thing:

> Have you seen but a bright lily grow
>   Before rude hands have touched it?
> Ha' you marked but the fall o' the snow
>   Before the soil hath smutched it?
> Ha' you felt the wool o' the beaver
>   Or swan's down ever?
> Or ha' smelt o' the bud o' the brier?
>   Or the nard in the fire?
> Or have tasted the bag of the bee?
> O so white! O so soft! O so sweet is she!

For my money this is more directly sensual than anything by the Stratford writer, but it is created in stillness. From the beginning we have the physical sensation of the woman, and we go on experiencing her sensually. She never becomes something else or stands for something else. There is no metamorphosis, no metaphor. The sight, touch, smell and taste of the woman are compared with the sight, touch, smell and taste of objects in nature. The physical in terms of the physical. When Shakespeare says:

> Shall I compare thee to a summer's day?

he is only vaguely conveying the physical sensation of the loved one. The boy he is addressing in the sonnet is beautiful, but what he felt, tasted, smelt like we shall never know. Presumably Shakespeare didn't either or, if he did, didn't choose to tell us. The boy is not like a summer's day, he is more lovely and more temperate. There is no direct correspondence between the boy and nature. He is an idealised form and cannot be described—or bedded. The writer is only concerned with what the writer can see—the beauty of the boy; and feel—his love for him and the endurance of his poetry. Time is devouring insistently, as it always is in

Shakespeare, but the abstractions will remain. Shakespeare's violets 'corrupt with virtuous season', his lilies 'fester', while Jonson's stay ever fresh as long as rude hands don't touch them. Time is not a factor for him; his writing remains of the earth, in a fixed moment and place, in the bodies and physical desires of his characters. With Shakespeare we are here and everywhere, *hic et ubique*, restlessly seeking and philosophising, taking us away from this too, too solid flesh. At the end of *The Tempest*, Prospero rejects not only the brute body of Caliban but the spirit of Ariel as well. Perhaps it is a mind only that sails back to Milan.

13
Language as Subject Matter

In the theatre the uneducated ear of a modern audience finds most Shakespeare artificial and, with the shrinking of the average person's vocabulary, obscure. They cannot tell whether it is good poetry, only that it doesn't sound like everyday speech. Does it matter whether it is good poetry (or prose)? Just ask, 'Is it an imaginative and accurate use of words by this character in this situation?' And for the actor, 'What do we know of the character at this moment in the play from the way it is written?' You should be able to tell from the language whether the character is sincere, fulsome, heartfelt, pedantic, devious, hysterical, bombastic or honest. It may even be meant to be boring. How long are the sentences, are there many subordinate clauses, how many adjectives are used, have the words one syllable or more, is the syntax fluid and shaped or jerky and awkward? (I leave aside the whole question of imagery.) A scrutiny of the style may provide answers to characterisation, as significant as analysis of motivation and circumstances.

Sometimes language itself becomes the subject matter. In *Love's Labour's Lost*, one of Shakespeare's earliest plays, he is obsessed with the way people speak, how language conceals pretension and evasion. Costard, the country clown, realises that the five-syllable word 'remuneration' is the way the impoverished aristocrat Don Adriano de Armado conceals the pitifully small tip he gives him. Words are used to create social status and establish superiority, or, like a Masonic code, to identify equality. In the following dialogue there is a bit of both. Armado is talking to Holofernes, the schoolmaster:

> ARMADO. Arts man, preambulate. We will be singled from the barbarous. Do you not educate youth at the charge house on the top of the mountain?
>
> HOLOFERNES. Or *mons*, the hill.
>
> ARMADO. At your sweet pleasure, for the mountain.
>
> HOLOFERNES. I do, sans question.
>
> ARMADO. Sir, it is the King's most sweet pleasure and affection to congratulate the Princess at her pavilion in the posteriors of this day, which the rude multitude call the afternoon.
>
> HOLOFERNES. The posterior of the day, most generous sir, is liable, congruent, and measurable for the afternoon. The word is well culled, chose, sweet and apt, I do assure you, sir, I do assure.

(Love's Labour's Lost 5.1)

And so they go on. They are happy to indulge each other's pedantry while affirming their own. Holofernes uses more Latin and foreign languages, otherwise their language is similar. Later we see Armado with the serving girl, Jacquenetta, when, through their relationship, he becomes a more rounded character. Unlike Dickens, Shakespeare never stereotypes the language of his characters so firmly that they cannot have an emotional life, nor are they as circumscribed as Jonson's characters. The puritanism of Malvolio is not the puritanism of Zeal-of-the-Land Busy or Tribulation Wholesome in Jonson's plays. Malvolio is a comic figure but he rejects the idea of reincarnation and thinks 'nobly of the soul'. Shakespeare's Shylock is more three-dimensional than Marlowe's Jew of Malta. Think of the wonderful passage of poetry that is given to Caliban, the monster, 'The isle is full of noises'. Every stereotype has the possibility of a more imaginative life.

The first Polonius I saw was that of Miles Malleson, the actor of wobbling chins and goggle eyes. He played him as was usual at that time (1944) as a comic buffoon. In the new orthodoxy, Polonius is a shrewd and cunning politician. (The new orthodoxy includes such insights as: Goneril and Regan are abused girls, Ophelia is well balanced and highly sexed, Prospero is a colonial exploiter, etc., etc.) To arrive at a true assessment of a character, look at what they do (and the way they do it) and what they say (and the way they say it). What does Polonius do? Are his actions those of a shrewd and cunning man? He completely misreads the cause of Hamlet's madness and refuses to be convinced of any alternative; he fails to see that he is being made fun of by Hamlet; he hides behind the arras, panics and gets himself killed. How does he talk? At length and with tiresome repetition and circumlocution and some pedantry ('More matter with less art,' the Queen says, but it doesn't stop him). And what does he say? Well, that's different. Many conventional and trite things, but interspersed with some pure gold:

> This above all: to thine own self be true,
> And it must follow, as the night the day,
> Thou canst not then be false to any man.

We have a man who cannot be dismissed as a buffoon but nor is he a clever political operator. All you have to do is read the text. The characterisation in the writing is so exact that it is difficult for the actor to go wrong. (When did you see a bad Polonius?) The Nurse in *Romeo and Juliet* is another flawless piece of character writing. It's almost impossible for it to miss in performance. With the Nurse, the unexpected character element is her advice to Juliet to conceal her marriage to Romeo and marry Paris—when the jolly, warm-hearted woman is shown to be corrupt and cynical.

Literary style does not only define character. In Shakespeare character is seldom divorced from situation and the writing reflects this. Sometimes it is used as part of the movement of the play, sometimes it marks emotional changes in the character (if these two can ever be separated). In *Twelfth Night* Viola starts her prepared speech to Olivia:

> Most radiant, exquisite and unmatchable beauty…

Olivia and her ladies laugh, and Viola justifies herself:

> Alas, I took great pains to study it, and 'tis poetical.

So we know what 'poetical' means—three adjectives where one would do. The first part of the scene in *Twelfth Night* is in prose, sophisticated banter, until Viola is left alone with Olivia and speaks from the heart in verse. The language becomes simpler with a new depth of feeling:

> Make me a willow cabin at your gate,
> And call upon my soul within the house…

By the time Viola leaves, Olivia has fallen in love and is committed to verse.

Later, Andrew Aguecheek overhears Viola talking to Olivia:

> VIOLA. Most excellent accomplished lady, the heavens
>   rain odours on you.
> SIR ANDREW. That youth's a rare courtier: 'rain odours',
>   well.
> VIOLA. My matter hath no voice, lady, but to your own
>   pregnant and vouchsafed ear.
> SIR ANDREW. 'Odours', 'pregnant' and 'vouchsafed'; I'll
>   get 'em all three already.

We know that Viola's choice of words is not from the heart, but they do have a certain splendour. At least Sir Andrew thinks so.

When Polonius reads Hamlet's letter to Ophelia aloud, he comments on it:

> 'To the celestial and my soul's idol, the most beautified
>   Ophelia—'

> That's an ill phrase, a vile phrase; beautified is a vile
> phrase.

and we are surely meant to agree that 'beautified Ophelia' is
artificial, just as we think it's typical of Polonius to repeat 'a
vile phrase'. He then reads this poem:

> 'Doubt thou the stars are fire,
>   Doubt that the sun doth move;
> Doubt truth to be a liar,
>   But never doubt I love.'

which is as cheap a piece of doggerel as you are likely to get.
We know that Hamlet in his daily speech makes better verse
than that. Its very badness calls in doubt the depth of his
feelings about Ophelia. In the graveyard scene he says:

> I loved Ophelia. Forty thousand brothers
> Could not, with all their quantity of love,
> Make up my sum.

But we are sceptical. Shakespeare has left it rather late in the
day, and the words do not ring true.

In the middle of the 'rogue and peasant slave' soliloquy
after the 'bloody, bawdy villain' outburst, Hamlet stops and
describes his own language:

> Why, what an ass am I? Ay, sure, this is most brave,
> That I, the son of the dear murderèd,
> Prompted to my revenge by heaven and hell,
> Must, like a whore, unpack my heart with words
> And fall a-cursing like a very drab,
> A scullion.

Using too many adjectives, particularly if they are
alliterative—'bloody, bawdy'—or rhyming—'treacherous,
lecherous'—is fit only for servants and prostitutes. 'I will
show how down-to-earth and purposeful I am by very
common language: 'whore', 'drab', 'scullion'. But we should
not fall into the trap of believing, as George Orwell did,
that all polysyllables are bad and all monosyllables good. (It's

no more true than that all polysyllables are of Latin origin and all monosyllables of Anglo-Saxon.) After the murder of Duncan, Macbeth says:

> Will all great Neptune's ocean wash this blood
> Clean from my hand? No, this my hand will rather
> The multitudinous seas incarnadine,
> Making the green one red.

The two rolling polysyllables are extravagantly baroque compared with the simple 'blood', 'hand', 'clean', 'green', 'red', but the contrast is surely intended, and it works. However, by the end of the banquet scene, the monosyllables have won the day:

> It will have blood, they say. Blood will have blood.

Sometimes Shakespeare is in the business of literary criticism. Marlowe's *Tamburlaine* was the great success of the rival theatre company. Its hero shouts as he enters the stage in a chariot drawn by the Kings of Trebizon and Soria, with bits in their mouths.

> Holla, ye pampered jades of Asia!
> What, can ye draw but twenty miles a day,
> And have so proud a chariot at your heels,
> And such a coachman as great Tamburlaine?

By the time Shakespeare wrote the second part of *Henry IV* this kind of rhetoric has become the rant of the braggart Pistol, in a tavern brawl with a whore.

> Shall pack-horses
> And hollow pampered jades of Asia,
> Which cannot go but thirty miles a day,
> Compare with Caesar and with cannibals,
> And Trojan Greeks?
> Nay, rather damn them with King Cerberus,
> And let the welkin roar.

This is not just the creation of a comic character but a questioning of heroic writing and perhaps heroism itself.

Most wonderful of all is the writing of Falstaff, in the first part of the same play in which he impersonates first the King, Hal's father, and then Hal himself. Mistress Quickly is laughing so much that she cries and Falstaff says:

> Weep not, sweet Queen, for trickling tears are vain.

Quickly recognises an end-stopped iambic pentameter when she hears it and laughs more. Falstaff caps it with:

> For God's sake, lords, convey my tristful Queen
> For tears do stop the floodgates of her eyes.

The writer is saying, 'I can write like that, but isn't it ridiculous?' This ironic critique of language has the same effect as the alternation of verse and prose. The heroic is undercut by the prosaic. The relation between the two suggests a synthesis.

Iago speaks in prose in his scenes with Roderigo and in an undecorated verse with Othello; Othello restrains his imagery when he is performing before his white masters but the language becomes richer as the emotions take over. When Iago has succeeded in setting the jealousy in motion he takes over the exotic style. It is as if he actually possesses Othello, or is possessed by him.

> Not poppy nor mandragora,
> Nor all the drowsy syrups of the world,
> Shall ever medicine thee to that sweet sleep
> Which thou owedst yesterday.

> *(Othello* 3.3)

The examples multiply. The use of language is always for dramatic or comic effect, never for beauty. They are markings for the actor.

14
Verse and Prose—*Hamlet* Again

A well-known dramatic critic said of a production of *Much Ado About Nothing* that the verse-speaking was poor, unaware that half the play was written in prose. Some actors believe that to play Shakespeare you have to learn to speak verse, assuming that all Shakespeare is written in verse. If they think about prose at all they would be surprised, like Molière's M. Jourdain, to find that they were speaking it all time. Prose is everyday speech and there is some magic device by which language is 'heightened' to become poetry. Poetry is different. The opposite tendency in verse-speaking today is to reverse the process and make poetry sound as much like ordinary speech as possible. It must be made 'real'. Well, some poetry sounds like ordinary speech anyway.

T.S. Eliot wrote about the first scene in *Hamlet*:

> The first twenty-two lines are built of the simplest
> words in the most homely idiom... No poet has begun
> to master dramatic verse until he has begun to write
> lines which, like these in *Hamlet*, are transparent. You
> are consciously attending not to the poetry, but to the
> meaning of the poetry. If you were hearing *Hamlet* for
> the first time, without knowing anything about the play,
> I do not think it would occur to you to ask whether the
> speakers were speaking in verse or prose.
>
> (*Poetry and Drama*)

Eliot was determined to rediscover the secret of dramatic writing for his own time. All previous poets, particularly those in the nineteenth century, had failed disastrously in their use of blank verse. All poets dream of rediscovering the secret of dramatic verse. Eliot came very near to understanding the problem. Unfortunately his own search for a dramatic transparency resulted in verse plays which are unimaginative and unpoetic. His later plays from *The Cocktail Party* onwards would have been better written in lively prose.

Unrhymed blank verse can be just an aid to speaking quickly and is not necessarily more poetic than any other form of writing. Prose can be imaginative and verse can be pedestrian. Both can be rhythmic and both can be rhetorical. An actor must learn to speak both and see them as equally expressive. In the melting pot of Shakespeare's experiment with theatre language they coexisted and were used at will. Is it beautiful poetry or elegant prose? Shakespeare didn't care. He probably never thought of his plays as literature; they only became so after his death. It was the actors who were 'the abstract and brief chronicles of the time', not the writer; a list of their names, including Shakespeare's, appears at the front of the First Folio. We are led by the inescapable fact that our greatest poet chose to write *plays*. That is, if he is our greatest poet. Would he still be thought so if he had only written the Sonnets, *Venus and Adonis* and *The Rape of Lucrece*? Probably not.

There is a pernicious habit of using the Sonnets as the starting point for actors speaking Shakespeare. But an actor needs to feel that something is happening dramatically through the language, and the Sonnets, by their nature, are not dynamic, they do not move. The poet is at a point in time. He looks at his experience and how he got there. Shakespeare's sonnets are about his personal life but they do not embody it. The subject of a tired ageing man working himself up over a good-looking boy is more successfully dramatised in the relation of Falstaff and Prince Hal in the two parts of *Henry IV*.

As a general rule in sixteenth-century drama, prose is more often used by lower classes, comics, madmen; verse by the nobility. Shakespeare as always started to break the rules.

Peter Hall sees it differently:

> It is always a shock to realise that Shakespeare's verse is his quickest and leanest means of communication. His verse does not represent 'poetics'. It is not poetry: for him it is the equivalent of ordinary speech. Artificiality is expressed by prose—it is always more formal, antithetical and ornate. The prose may also be the wrong-headed colloquialisms of Bottom and Dogberry as they strive for educated speech. But it can as well express the pretentious thought patterns of Don Armado. It is never natural speech: it is artificial. Natural speech is portrayed by the verse—economical, fleet, often using the simplest of words...
>
> *(Exposed by the Mask)*

In his desire to insist on the naturalness of verse Hall goes too far. Bottom and Dogberry are in prose because they are meant to be funny, and it is easier to be funny in prose. But there are plenty of examples of fluent prose and clunking verse. Hamlet's 'What a piece of work is a man' is in prose. It is never 'formal, antithetical or ornate'; its language is simple and direct. Nor is verse always leaner. There is no rule of thumb. All the writing is meant to sound like people talking to each other, though I doubt whether Shakespeare, or his audience, ever thought it was the 'equivalent of ordinary speech', a concept of a more democratic age.

By the time of *Hamlet*, whose central character may or may not be mad, but anyway is pretending to be, the divisions are breaking down. He speaks both verse and prose. A noble character who is also mad. In what form should he express himself? In one scene alone, the arrival of the Players, we are taken through a variety of prose and verse. The scene starts with Hamlet baiting Polonius in prose; Rosencrantz and Guildenstern arrive and the prose continues, very down-to-earth, fast, clever undergraduate chat. Hamlet, still talking prose, attempts to explain his melancholy:

> What a piece of work is a man, how noble in reason,
> how infinite in faculties, in form and moving how
> express and admirable, in action how like an angel, in
> apprehension how like a god; the beauty of the world,
> the paragon of animals; and yet to me, what is this
> quintessence of dust? Man delights not me; nor woman
> neither, though by your smiling you seem to say so.

The Players arrive and speak prose but are coaxed, without too much difficulty, into giving us 'a taste of their quality' in conventional blank verse, in a speech from a play about the Trojan War. We can tell it's old-fashioned because it doesn't sound like anything we have heard so far:

> The rugged Pyrrhus, he whose sable arms,
> Black as his purpose, did the night resemble
> When he lay couchèd in th' ominous horse
> Hath now this dread and black complexion smeared
> With heraldry more dismal. Head to foot
> Now is he total gules, horridly tricked
> With blood of fathers, mothers, daughters, sons,
> Baked and impasted with the parching streets
> That lend a tyrannous and damnèd light
> To their lord's murder.

The words thud down in regular iambics, and the lines do not flow one into another but in their own way are effective. The speech uses a sustained metaphor from heraldry and works it through to excess: 'Head to foot now is he total gules' has a kind of splendid baroque flourish which verges on the comic. Yet Hamlet speaks it with relish and earlier has praised the writer as being free from affectation and for a specialised taste, with scenes 'set down with as much modesty as cunning'. Can he be serious? Perhaps Shakespeare/

Hamlet secretly wanted to write in this style but had a more complex and searching task. After the Players leave there is a brief bridge of:

Ay, so God bye to you. Now I am alone.

before he launches into:

O, what a rogue and peasant slave am I

—vivid, exaggerated but passionate verse quite unlike the majestic controlled writing of the 'rugged Pyrrhus'. But it too has its excesses:

Bloody, bawdy villain!
Remorseless, treacherous, lecherous, kindless villain!
O vengeance!

But as we saw earlier, Hamlet stops himself and criticises his own style and diction. The scene ends in a simple couplet:

The play's the thing
Wherein I'll catch the conscience of the King.

Later in the play, while the actors prepare to stage *The Murder of Gonzago*, Hamlet, in his very colloquial prose, tells them how to act. When the play itself begins we might expect something not unlike the 'rugged Pyrrhus', with Hamlet's interpolation, perhaps played in the style dictated by Hamlet in his advice. Do we get it? No, we are given something naive in rhyming couplets, more like a mummers' play.

Full thirty times hath Phoebus' cart gone round
Neptune's salt wash and Tellus' orbèd ground
And thirty dozen moons with borrowed sheen
About the world have times twelve thirties been…

In fact we never know which bit, if any, is Hamlet's interpolation.

When the play explodes the situation and Claudius leaves, Hamlet's language disintegrates as a means of coherent communication.

Why let the stricken deer go weep
The hart ungallèd play
For some must watch while some must sleep
So runs the world away.

No one, least of all Hamlet, knows what it means. Poetry becomes meaningless doggerel. We are watching a kind of breakdown. The success of his plan to unmask the King has left him with real responsibility for his action, and he cannot face it. The personality starts to crumble with the writing. Coherence returns in the scene of prose dialogue with Rosencrantz and Guildenstern about the recorders. It is a scene of breathtaking speed. The wit which had formerly been a protection is now an aggressive weapon. But the transition to wit at a moment when action should follow is an evasion. Hamlet is left alone, and we are plunged into crude melodramatic verse which bears no relation to what has gone before:

'Tis now the very witching time of night
When churchyards yawn, and hell itself breathes out
Contagion to this world. Now could I drink hot blood
And do such bitter business as the day
Would quake to look on.

Who does he think he is kidding? This is bad, over-the-top rant and the writer knows it. Hamlet is a long way from drinking hot blood, and the only bitter business is giving his mother a telling-off, not killing his murdering uncle.

Throughout the play Hamlet's poetry and prose keep changing and, like Macbeth, the style towards the end becomes simpler and less hysterical with the character's resignation and acceptance of death. The writing is indicative of inner psychology without its being directly expressed. Poetry in the theatre is the resonance that takes us outside the particular predicament of the character to relate it to larger issues, the natural world, to society as a whole, and in so doing makes us look at the character from the outside.

It can also give the actor some awareness of the existence
of his part beyond personal psychology. Most of the above
is routine literary criticism, but of what use is it to the actor?
Many actors think that everything they speak is an expression of what their characters think and feel—and, in a
sense, it is. But being aware that a passage is more
overblown or exaggerated will give an insight into the character as seen from the outside. An actor can criticise or
comment on his character without losing his identity in the
action. This is key for his understanding. Some actors think
that all they need to do is feel, and the words will look after
themselves. There is an equally false belief that the words
will do it all for you. Words have to be allowed to do their
work, but they must seem to come from the character and
situation. It's difficult with an old play where all the language
may seem strange and artificial, but it's a director's job, as
far as he or she can, to help the actor to understand what
might have been near conversational in its own period and
what would have sounded artificial.

Any tips for the actor? Don't be overawed by the text but
look at it carefully on the page. The only real difference
between verse and prose is that one is laid out in lines and
the other isn't. Try and see the shape of the speech and how
it might affect your speaking. Only by speaking aloud will
you feel the stress and rhythm of the writing, whether in
verse or prose. I deal with this in a later chapter.

15
The Words of Puritans—Shaw and Bunyan

Shakespeare had little of the puritan in him, either morally or linguistically, though in Malvolio he draws a not entirely unsympathetic picture of one. But the killjoy nature of puritanism is fixed for all time by this:

> SIR TOBY (*to* MALVOLIO). Dost thou think because thou art virtuous there shall be no more cakes and ale?
>
> FESTE. Yes, by Saint Anne, and ginger shall be hot in the mouth too.

George Bernard Shaw, a self-confessed puritan, knew Shakespeare inside out but professed to despise him for portraying worthless, reactionary, non-visionary people who would never change the world. He compares him unfavourably to Bunyan as a stylist.

> Even in mere technical adaptation to the art of the actor, Bunyan's dramatic speeches are as good as Shakespeare's tirades. Only a trained dramatic speaker can appreciate the terse manageableness and effectiveness of such a speech as this… 'By this I perceive thou art one of my subjects; for all that country is mine, and I am the Prince and the God of it. How is it then that thou hast run away from thy King? Were it not that I hope thou mayst do me more service, I would strike thee now at one blow to the ground.' Here there is no raving and swearing and rhyming and classical allusion. The sentences go straight to their mark; and their concluding phrases soar like the sunrise,

or swing and drop like a hammer, just as the actor
wants them.

(from the Saturday Review, January 1897)

Shakespeare is full of raving and swearing. All his tragic
heroes overstate their case. Hamlet says he could drink hot
blood—but doesn't; Othello says he will chop Desdemona
into messes, but only strangles her; Macbeth wants great
Neptune's oceans to wash the blood from his hand—and
so on. They all go well over the top. Lear can't even find the
words:

> I will do such things, what they are I know not
> But they shall be the terrors of the earth.

But all these characters have a foil, a conflicting voice which
will offer common sense to put their extravagance into per-
spective, expressed in prose or in basic unemotional
language: Iago for Othello, Lady Macbeth for Macbeth, and
so on. My favourite is in *Antony and Cleopatra* where the
lovers try to outdo each other in hyperbole. When Antony
is dead, Cleopatra has a succession of exaggerated speeches
in his praise. She finishes with:

> Think you there was or might be such a man
> As this I dreamt of?

And the very minor character of Dolabella answers:

> Gentle madam, no.

This juxtaposition between characters and between styles
of writing is unique and rich. Did Shakespeare sometimes
identify with his characters, was he intoxicated by his own
exuberance, by his emotional, rhetorical, imaginative ability?
Perhaps, but his constant ability to offset the rhetoric brings
himself and the play down to earth.

Bunyan's phrases are wonderful and speakable, but it is
impossible to imagine a whole play written at that level. It
is a direct statement of strength and goodness. Bunyan was

not interested in character or the nature of corruption, but only the right actions which lead to salvation. Shaw never understood the darkness in people and their potential for evil. He could not identify with them so he could not write them. He thought the Fascist dictators were joke figures and portrayed them as such in his play *Geneva*. He was not a poet and did not understand the nature of poetry, which is shown in his writing of the poet, Marchbanks, in *Candida*. The idea that the style of the writing would change with character and situation was alien to him. There is no sub-text in Shaw but there's not much passion either.

Puritans have never liked the theatre. In 1642 the approach of the Civil War closed all the theatres and they remained firmly closed during the Protectorate and didn't reopen until 1660. In the gap many things changed: the plays, with their new influences from Paris, the ways of presenting drama, the shape of the buildings—and the language had changed too. The Puritan Revolution banned drama but did not prevent poetry being written. Two of the greatest poets of the seventeenth century, Milton and Marvell, worked as Cromwell's secretaries. The great river of English poetry surged on in spite of political change, absorbed it and was part of it. But it had lost the basic sensuality of Ben Jonson.

In drama there was a more disruptive break. Shakespeare's wonderful variety was rejected. No longer could comic elements enter the purity of classical tragedy. Comedy and tragedy became separate entities. Comedies, about contemporary life, were written in prose, and heroic tragedies, about historical or mythical characters, in verse. Comedy and tragedy, verse and prose were never again to be united. The only plays of post-Restoration drama to be revived in our own time have been comedies, from Etherege to Noël Coward. (The only Restoration tragedy occasionally revived is Otway's *Venice Preserv'd*, and that only because it has two scenes of sadomasochism.) The high moral principles on which tragedy is based quickly become laughable to a succeeding age, even when they are no longer written in verse. After the Restoration, characters could no longer express powerful emotions truthfully. Plays of any quality were about people's social behaviour and their concealment of emotion, and this lasted well into the twentieth century. Nothing in our life is noble enough for tragedy.

16
Action and Imagination—*Macbeth*

The action of *Macbeth* is fast. The play is half the length of *Hamlet*. The scenes are short and move the action forward. And yet somehow it allows time for an imaginative life for its protagonist which gives the play its character. The language in the play is not witty and intellectually challenging like *Hamlet* and there is very little prose. Macbeth is a better poet than Hamlet, or rather he swims in poetry as his natural medium. He doesn't need prose. Everything he feels he expresses. He is not struggling with his own identity but with action and its consequences. Compared with Hamlet, Macbeth is a man who does things, a great warrior who has just won the war and is admired by everybody, but we only see him after the battle, transfixed by the witches' prophecy. When he returns to his wife it is she who drives the action while he is very passive and hesitant. After the King's arrival at Glamis we hear Macbeth's doubts about the murder, not so much because he feels it to be wrong but because it will produce pity in the whole world:

> Besides, this Duncan
> Hath borne his faculties so meek, hath been
> So clear in his great office, that his virtues
> Will plead like angels, trumpet-tongued, against
> The deep damnation of his taking off;
> And Pity, like a naked new-born babe,
> Striding the blast, or heaven's Cherubin, horsed
> Upon the sightless couriers of the air,

Shall blow the horrid deed in every eye,
That tears shall drown the wind.

And we are astonished not so much by the intensity of feeling but by the extravagance of the poetic imagination.
There is a wonderful picture by Blake called *Pity*, which
attempts to render this image in visual form.

After Macbeth has agreed to commit the murder he waits
for the bell which is his wife's signal. He sees the dagger in
the air drawing him to the murder. We don't see it but we
see him see it, our imagination is now part of his. We don't
know whether it attracts or repels him. Is it real or not? He
tries to touch it without success. He dismisses it from his
mind, which immediately moves on to other images:

> Now o'er the one half-world
> Nature seems dead, and wicked dreams abuse
> The curtained sleep. Witchcraft celebrates
> Pale Hecate's offerings, and withered Murder...

and we are off on a journey with him, moving through the
night, like Scrooge and the Ghosts of Christmas, looking at
other wrongdoers, at the personified Murder, moving like
the rapist Tarquin, like a ghost. The actor is there, on the
stage, but his words have released us to an imaginary world.
We are brought back to the physical here and now, and Macbeth has become the figure of the Murder he is about to
commit. He talks to the ground he is about to walk on. He
is still. The bell rings.

> I go and it is done. The bell invites me.

His imagination has created the dagger to move him to the
murder, and his own poetry has turned him into the
murderer.

The stage is empty for a moment; then his wife comes on. Her
speech covers the tension we feel; is the deed being done... or
not? We hear Macbeth shout offstage. What has happened? I

know of nothing more exciting and simply theatrical than this and the scene that follows. Macbeth reappears and is greeted with 'My husband?'—a question that implies, 'Are you the man I married, are you worthy to share my bed?'

> MACBETH. I have done the deed. Didst thou not hear a noise?
>
> LADY MACBETH. I heard the owl scream and the crickets cry.
> Did not you speak?
>
> MACBETH. When?
>
> LADY MACBETH. Now.
>
> MACBETH. As I descended?
>
> LADY MACBETH. Ay.
>
> MACBETH. Hark! Who lies in the second chamber?
>
> LADY MACBETH. Donalbain.
>
> MACBETH. This is a sorry sight.
>
> LADY MACBETH. A foolish thought to say a sorry sight.

The short lines express the shared tension of the couple. Macbeth tells of the two men and his inability to say 'Amen' and then begins his elaborate invocation of sleep:

> Sleep, that knits up the ravelled sleave of care,
> The death of each day's life, sore labour's bath,
> Balm of hurt minds, great Nature's second course,
> Chief nourisher in life's feast...

His wife interrupts him—'What do you mean?'—but she can't stop the outpouring. They both speak in verse but everything, she says is prosaic and practical.

> There are two lodged together... Who was it that thus cried?... Give me the daggers... I hear a knocking at the south entry... A little water clears us of this deed... Get on your nightgown...

She uses hardly any imagery. The gap between her language and his is huge, but it is still two people talking. Their words take us in and out of their minds, setting up ideas whose importance they are unaware of. Three of the main themes of the play—the blood as the symbol of guilt; the inability of the guilty to sleep; and the consequences of action—are all introduced naturally, dramatically and with the utmost economy, without in any way impeding the flow of the action. Lady Macbeth rejects the emotion and the poetry, but the images stay with her. She has to behave like a sensible teacher or a doctor, but everything her husband says sinks into her mind and stays in her unconscious till it reappears in the sleepwalking scene. Then she needs the doctor.

The invocation of sleep is hysterical and overwrought. Frank Kermode called it fustian, and so it may be, but it is splendid fustian. It is as if the murder had opened Macbeth's poetic bowels. At the end of the scene he is an apparent wreck incapable of action. But he has become the deed's creature and we never see him as craven again. Later he goes with the other lords to see Duncan's body, in spite of having said he was too scared, and kills the two grooms, justifying it in this speech:

> Here lay Duncan,
> His silver skin laced with his golden blood,
> And his gashed stabs looked like a breach in nature
> For ruin's wasteful entrance.

Which is run-of-the-mill conventional poetry. It lacks conviction but it has a certain facile deviousness. His wife, being no literary critic, mistakes it for the beginning of a hysterical breakdown and faints. From this point on he is in charge and no longer needs her. He has become desensitised. He is still a poet, but the kind of poetry changes, and he proceeds to increasingly violent and reckless action. He reacts to Banquo's ghost with another flood of rhetoric but it has a demented courage; at the end of the scene he even manages some humour:

> The time has been
> That when the brains were out the man would die,
> And there an end; but now they rise again
> With twenty mortal murders on their crowns,
> And push us from our stools.

And the diction has altered:

> It will have blood, they say. Blood will have blood.
> Stones have been known to move and trees to speak...

By the end of the play he has supped full with horrors. He is not less poetic but the form, the vocabulary is different. The language of 'Tomorrow and tomorrow and tomorrow' is spare, the imagery simple and compressed and the rhetorical development economical. Macbeth's journey through the play is between his actions in the real world and his imagination. Mark Antony's rhetoric in the Forum created the actions that followed it. Macbeth's poetry is a response to his own actions. He is an evil monster but we cannot avoid being part of—or at least fascinated witnesses of—this journey.

17
Stress, Metre and Pitch

English is an accented language. Changing the accent in a word can change its meaning—*en*trance/en*trance*, con*vict/convict*, *re*fuse/re*fuse* and so on. It must be hell for foreigners. Speaking any text, verse or prose, you accent the word that you think makes the line clear, or rather you make a line clear and find you have stressed one word more than another. Many actors underline in their scripts the word they mean to stress. A straight, flat little line under the word is like a metal weight pulling the word down, or a foot pushing it into the ground. If you suggest to actors that the stress they have chosen may be misguided, they squash down another word, instead of rethinking the whole sentence. Whenever I read a piece of prose in which the writer has italicised particular words—Lewis Carroll is an example—I cannot speak the line in my head. My voice moves along the line and is suddenly brought up short by this block rearing up in front of me. It's like Ayers Rock in the middle of the desert. I can't get over it and I can't go round it. When I stress the word so that it isolates itself from the rest of the sentence it sounds wrong. I am sure that is not how Carroll heard it in his head. The rise and fall around the stressed word often subtly affects the meaning, just as one hill is only slightly higher than another in a range. Discussions of the important word in a sentence in isolation are unproductive, unless the shape of the whole sentence is tested with it. It is more important to think of a line as a unit in which the outcome of the whole suggests the stress. (This might be one good reason for actioning a line.)

Stresses in classical languages are short or long, but in English they are usually light or strong, whether in verse or prose. I prefer 'light' to 'weak', and 'strong' to 'heavy'. 'Weak' and 'heavy' are negative words. Nowadays much speech does indeed consist of heavy stress, which drags the line down. 'Light' and 'strong' suggests a springiness in which even the less important words have life. In 'the cat sat on the mat', 'sat' and 'mat' are likely to take a stronger stress than 'the' and 'on', whatever the intention behind the line. The line is a statement of fact: the cat was sitting on the mat. (It could also mean, with the ambiguity of the English language, that the cat sat down on the mat.) The line is without a speaker and without a context. Like a messenger's speech in Greek tragedy it is impersonal.

As a general rule the following take lighter stresses:

- Articles
- Prepositions
- Most pronouns
- Conjunctions

The following take stronger stresses:
- Verbs—except auxiliary verbs
- Nouns

Adjectives and adverbs are variable.

Light stresses must never be thrown away. The patterns made between light and strong form the basis of speech. If the patterns become regular, the speech becomes verse. The word order in English, with the articles—'a', 'an', 'the'— before the noun, makes a natural pattern of light before strong, which in verse is called an iamb. (Aristotle thought that the iambic form was the most like real speech.) Two light stresses before a strong—anapest—is also common. 'The cat' is iambic, 'on the mat' is anapestic. But it is iambic which is the basis of most English verse and in the form of five iambics together (pentameter), usually unrhymed, it is the basis of the plays of Shakespeare and his contemporaries. The strong stress is the basis of the divisions of the line into feet but it is the relation of light to strong which makes the rhythm.

'To be or not to be; that is the question' is an iambic line but it's not entirely regular. (For one thing it has an extra syllable, but I don't want to go into that at the moment.) Regular stress would demand that 'is' should be strong and that doesn't sound right. It would seem more natural to take the stronger stress on 'that' which makes a dum-da rather than a da-dum (this is called a trochee). The reversing of the stress in the middle of the line highlights the word 'that'. This does not mean that it has to be spoken with any extra emphasis; the metrical break has already given it emphasis. A trochee is particularly effective at the beginning of a line that is otherwise iambic. The Chorus begins *Henry V* with 'O, for a muse of fire that would ascend / The brightest heaven of invention'. You have to start with a strong stress on 'O' and one on 'muse'. This 'strong-light-light-strong' on the first four syllables gives a forward thrust to the speech—and the whole play.

As a general rule always stress a line first for sense, and only in extreme cases go against sense to satisfy the demands of the metre (unlike singing where you go for metre first). Sometimes you have to use unusual stresses because a word was pronounced differently in the period in which it was written. In the following example, Cleopatra is saying what she would endure rather than be led in triumph through the streets of Rome:

> rather make
> My country's high Pyramides my gibbet
> And hang me up in chains.

(Antony and Cleopatra 5.2)

If you say 'Pyramides' with three syllables, stressed on the first as we would today, you get an irregular line with three light stresses together. You also have to pause between 'high' and 'Pyramides' to keep it in some sort of rhythm. I'm not sure that it is not preferable to the four-syllable 'py-*ram*-i-dees' with a strong stress on the second syllable, which correct metre demands. The latter sticks in the throat and most of the audience wouldn't know what you're talking about. You could justify it by saying it is a piece of typical overstatement by Cleopatra and will pass unnoticed in the flow of passion.

In his first meeting with the Ghost, Hamlet says:

> Let me not burst in ignorance, but tell
> Why thy canonised bones, hearsèd in death,
> Have burst their cerements, why the sepulchre
> Wherein we saw thee quietly inurned
> Hath oped his ponderous and marble jaws
> To cast thee up again.

> *(Hamlet* 1.5)

You have to stress 'canonised' on the second syllable and possibly in 'sepulchre' too; 'hearsèd' must have two syllables. The effect is of a baroque tomb, as elaborate as the one the Ghost has broken out of, conveying a bizarre splendour which justifies the strangeness of the speaking.

Analysis must never replace the ear as the guide to speaking. When I first worked at Stratford I was told by John Barton, one of the directors and an ex-academic, that the line in Richard III's first soliloquy—

> In the deep bosom of the ocean buried

—was a six-foot line with both 'ocean' and 'buried' being pronounced with three syllables. Just try it on the tongue. You know it doesn't work; it is undramatic. I ignored his advice. In fact if you stress the line simply for sense you end up with four stresses not five. Surely most actors say:

In the **deep bo**som of the ocean **buried**

In fact it is possible to feel the whole opening of the speech as made up of four-stress lines:

> **Now** is the **win**ter of our **dis**con**tent**
> Made **glo**rious **sum**mer by this **sun** of **York**
> And **all** the **smiles** that **lowered** upon our **house**
> In the **deep bo**som of the ocean **bur**ied

Even in *Hamlet* you can have a four-stress line:

> To **be** or **not** to be; **that** is the **ques**tion

That means you are looking at a line as made up of strong stresses with an irregular number of smaller stresses round them, which is neither iambic or trochaic. In fact it is more like Old English poetry. This has been argued before, and inconclusively. If it is carried through, as a general rule it starts to have an overemphatic, aggressive character, and loses some of the easy flow of the writing. I believe that the underlying pattern must be iambic and and that an actor will find the natural sense stress inside it. There is something about the iambic pentameter that keeps things moving. There are many gradations between light and strong, in which the difference between them starts to disappear. The actor must listen to his own voice.

Before committing yourself to an interpretation of a line, feel the sense running through it and avoid stressing any one word too heavily. Let the line develop its strength, don't drag it down or stamp it into the soil until it cannot move. Above all, avoid stressing too many words. Focus on the situation and character as far as you understand them. Don't use the line to commit yourself to an emotional statement until you know what the character is feeling, and even then try to let the line have a life of its own. Allow each sentence to flow easily to its end, trying to feel its structure on the way. If there are a number of sentences joined by a conjunction, or a sentence with many subordinate clauses, you may have to approach these as separate units, but the principle is the same.

As an exercise, try saying the whole speech beginning 'To be or not to be' without emphasis or variation of pitch and see what happens. You will find it's not possible, without an unnatural effort, to give equal value and maintain unvaried pitch. The tongue will start to give the lightest of stresses to 'be' rather than 'to', the voice will go very slightly up and down. You will feel the natural shape of the line and its possibilities.

This is how Olivier, who was not at home in moments of meditation, would approach the quieter parts of his text. He would relax all the facial muscles so that there was no tension anywhere; the eyes would roll up under the lids and the tongue dart in and out of his loose mouth like a lizard's; the delivery became clipped and impersonal as he gave nearly equal value to all the syllables. You can hear the effect in the soliloquy 'Upon the King…' in the film of *Henry V* (though there the voice is on the soundtrack and the face doesn't move). It may sound artificial but it is far preferable to injecting a heavy and false emotion by forcing the stress.

Nowadays strong stresses are used too frequently on television by politicians and salesmen (what's the difference?) and even academics. No one talks about anything in a civilised manner. Everyone is trying to hammer something into our thick skulls. In the process the natural alternation of light and strong gets lost, and so does the music. The weather forecasters are the worst. The autocue can only show a few words at a time so the speaker phrases without relation to sense and breathes when his breath runs out. This is often between verb and object, or between adjective and noun. The short breath is used to give a completely unnecessary stress to the word that follows. There is also an incomprehensible stressing of auxiliary words and conjunctions: speech is no longer made up of sentences in which the sense moves towards the full stop. The speaker only knows as much as he sees. This has now become a mannerism and is used by actors in drama, where there is no autocue and no need to take a breath.

Stressing conjunctions is a common fault. It gives a tired, heavy feel to speaking. 'There will be rain over England **and** Scotland,' or even 'England **and** (*short breath*) Scotland', as if this was an extra burden to bear, but this is belied by the cheerful tone in which it is said. At one time 'and' was so understressed that it would disappear almost entirely. 'Rock 'n' roll' or 'fish 'n' chips' are inseparable units. Rock and roll is, after all, one thing, and fish and chips nearly so. We used to fulminate against this elision in speaking as destroying the rhythm, which it did. In regular verse 'and' always counts as a syllable. Now it is given equally unrhythmic importance.

The famous *hendiadys* of Shakespeare (two words yoked together, of equal value and often of related meaning, governing a third) is built on the balance of the conjunction:

- The very age and body of the time his form and pressure
- This accident and flood of fortune
- The chief good and market of his time

If you stress 'and' you ruin the phrase. (No one has ever quite explained why Shakespeare was so addicted to this form. It does give a kind of detachment to what is often a passionate moment.)

The other monstrosity is the unnecessary stressing of personal pronouns, one of my personal *bêtes noires*. This is a major failing in actors who should know better. John Mills at Olivier's memorial service read the lesson:

Charity never faileth; but whether there be prophecies
    they shall fail;
whether there be tongues **they** shall cease;
whether there be knowledge **it** shall vanish away.

Even though 'fail' is repeated in the first line and it might seem sensible to stress 'they', the balance of the second and third line surely demands a pattern for the whole like this:

> Charity never faileth; but whether there be **prophecies**
>   they shall **fail**;
> whether there be **tongues** they shall **cease**;
> whether there be **knowledge** it shall **vanish away**.

—with a slightly stronger emphasis on the verbs at the ends of the lines. The phrase moves towards the verb for its fulfilment.

As a general rule never stress personal or possessive pronouns at the beginning of a line or phrase. It gives a ludicrously self-centred impression and is always unmusical.

> **Mine** eyes have seen the glory of the coming of the
>   Lord

is unthinkable. It is the seeing of the glory, not who sees it. Similarly:

> **I** know that my Redeemer liveth

—where the knowing of the livingness of the Redeemer is the only thing. The line is only complete when 'liveth' has been said. The awareness of the end of the line and the sense of moving towards it is the basis of all good speaking. Subject, verb and object are one and inseparable.

> I know that my Redeemer **liveth**.

The self does not exist apart from the actions it performs. The life and meaning of the action is what matters.

This would be unnecessary advice to a singer who knows that the flow, shape and rhythm are in the music, and that nothing must impede their progress. There is a film of Maria Callas singing a number of different arias at a concert—arias ranging from the heavy drama of Lady Macbeth to the comedy of Rosina in *The Barber of Seville*. Before each aria she has a moment of concentration in which her focus is on the new character and situation. Thereafter is only the music. The playwright's indications of rhythm, pace and phrasing are rarely as exact as a composer's (though I believe they are often more precise than an actor realises), but an actor can have something of the same sensation. He must experience an emotional impulse at the beginning which will energise the whole line. It must not be shoved along, stress by stress.

The text has a life to be released rather than something hugged to one's chest. I believe that dramatic writing has an existence which demands space to be released not just towards the other actors but outwards to a space which includes the audience. The text does not belong to the actor. This is a risky doctrine which could lead to a cold impersonality or even the worst excesses of ham acting, but without it there is no true theatre speaking.

The Use of Pitch

Variation of pitch is a form of stress that can be made without weight and is often more effective. It can be just as meaningful without slowing the pace. The iambic pentameter has a natural lift from the light stress to the strong. The lines move trippingly through the sense, and importance can be given without effort. Perhaps it belongs to a different age when the wit of a line was unfolded gracefully by the rise and fall of the voice, whether on stage or off. Now everything—or nothing—is conveyed by an aggressive downward stress, usually on the first word: 'GO (*pause*) AWAY' or 'DON'T (*pause*) DO THAT'. It is unmusical and inexpressive—and of course uniambic. Only in the regular and monotonous stress of rap is poetry possible. The nature of iambic verse is to lift, not to be pushed downwards.

It is essential in speaking a classic text to use pitch to clarify or emphasise meaning. A light and even delivery, where all the words have value, keeps the line moving; the pitch clarifies the sense. 'Speak the speech, I pray you, as I pronounce it to you trippingly on the tongue.'

The first actors' voices I knew well were those of John Gielgud (b. 1904) and Edith Evans (b. 1888). I include their dates because their approach seems to be moulded by their time. Both were born before the First World War but only Evans was acting before it started. I used to have scratchy old records of them reading an anthology called *The Voice of Poetry*, which consisted mainly of Shakespeare and the Romantics, and those poets we used to call Georgian from the period 1910 to 1935. Gielgud had been taught at RADA; Evans never went to a drama school but received her early training as an amateur, working with William Poel, the first director to explore a return to the stage of Shakespeare's time.

The dominant voice teacher of the time was Elsie Fogerty, the founder of the Central School of Speech and Drama, and, later, her pupil Gwynneth Thurburn. She taught Laurence Olivier and Peggy Ashcroft. One of the main principles of the time was a belief that the pitch should be lifted gradually over the length of a line and never dropped, except to complete the cadence of a final thought. Sometimes this became a mannerism. When Olivier finishes his 'Once more unto the breach' speech in his film of *Henry V*—

And upon this charge
Cry God for Harry, England and Saint Ge-e-e-orge

—he builds his climax by raising his pitch at such large intervals that the voice almost cracks on the last word and is only saved by the crash of sound from William Walton's score.

When Evans was playing Lady Bracknell in *The Importance of Being Earnest*, she would say (the dashes are mine to indicate the actor's phrasing):

> You can hardly imagine—that I and Lord Bracknell—
> would dream of allowing our only daughter—a girl
> brought up with the utmost care—to marry into a cloak
> room, and form an alliance with a parcel. Good
> morning, Mr Worthing.

She inexorably lifted the pitch by stages, through the line, to 'parcel' before she came down. In the same scene her much imitated and derided 'handbag' is built on an extreme interval between the two syllables, but it is also created by the intensity of 'ha-a-a-nd' before the release of 'bag'. The relation of power, intensity, richness of vowel with mobility of pitch was one of her great skills. Her use of an overall upward lift in speaking conveyed, amongst other things, a relentless optimism and a generous and all-embracing view of the world. There is an announcer on Radio 3 who constantly lifts her squeaky pitch on every third or fourth word but drops it again immediately on the next. She conveys a naturally depressive personality desperately trying to cheer herself up, without success. Evans was a Christian Scientist, determined to show that the world was good and healthy, which meant keeping her intonation up; just as, it is said, she would gaze at the reflection of her lopsided face in the mirror and say, 'I am beautiful.' Her vocal technique was part of her spiritual armoury.

Her use of pitch was quite conscious ('I have perfect pitch, you know'). In my production of *Richard III* at Stratford in 1961, Christopher Plummer as Richard would say to Evans playing Margaret:

> but I was born so high,
> Our eyrie buildeth in the cedar's top,
> And dallies with the wind and scorns the sun—

which she interrupts with:

> And turns the sun to shade. Alas, alas!
> Witness my son, now in the shade of death,
> Whose bright outshining beams thy cloudy wrath
> Hath in eternal darkness folded up.

Plummer would give her an upward inflection on 'scorns the sun' and she would say, 'No, Chris. You see I have to come over the top of your last word and if you pitch it up it's very hard for me.' But Plummer always went up and she always pitched above him. The effect was stunning. It was purely technical but in no way detracted from the emotion of the scene. In fact it helped to create it. This would not be true for American English where intensity, rather than pitch, is used to create emotion. British English has, or rather had, a natural rise and fall which, to the American ear, sounds affected, if not downright camp.

One old-fashioned trick, which can still work, was the sudden dropping of pitch to create an unexpected seriousness or sentimental depth. Gielgud tells us that Fred Terry as the Scarlet Pimpernel would drop his voice a whole octave when he said to his wife: 'I could never bear to see a pretty woman cry.' Edith Evans in *Daphne Laureola* by James Bridie realises her old husband is about to die and the voice leaves its soaring arabesques and drops right down as she says, 'Oh, Joe, don't go. I need you.' In my production of *The Way of the World*, Maggie Smith, in the famous scene between Millamant and Mirabell where they state their conditions for a good marriage, would drop her voice on the word 'lastly' as she made the proviso: 'And lastly, wherever I am, you shall always knock at the door before you come in.' On a line on which she could have easily got a laugh she chose to say to the audience 'Take this bit seriously', and so gave the scene an unexpected depth.

18
Magic and Metaphor—*The Tempest* and *Henry VIII*

You have just been to a new play and have to describe it to friends. They say, 'What's it about?' They partly mean, 'What happens in the play? What's the story? Who are the characters?' And partly 'What does the play add up to? What is the significance of the narrative? What does it mean?' The first questions can be answered clearly; the second are more difficult, and the two get intertwined. With an old play the 'What's it about?' is superseded by 'How do they do it?'— meaning 'What interpretative stress do they put on the narrative?' Plays mean different things at different times, and the narrative can yield possibilities undreamt of by the author. Our attitude to characters may change but the narrative is the constant to which any interpretation must be related. For instance, it is now a commonplace to think that *The Tempest* is a play 'about' colonialism. Let's remind ourselves of the narrative.

Prospero, the Duke of Milan, has become involved in his studies and neglected his dukedom. Antonio, his brother, ousts him in a coup, helped by the King of Naples. Prospero and his baby daughter are cast away in a boat and land on a desert island. When the play starts they have been living on the island for twelve years. Prospero, who has magical powers, has two servants: Ariel, 'an airy spirit' whom he has freed from imprisonment by a witch, and the witch's son, Caliban, 'a monster'. By chance Antonio and the King of Naples are sailing home from a wedding in

Tunis. Prospero creates a storm by magic and his enemies are shipwrecked on the island. By the end of the play he has forgiven them, and his daughter and the son of the King of Naples are united. He renounces his magic powers and returns to Milan as its Duke.

That misses out the comic subplot and the stages by which Prospero arrives at the realisation of his plan, but it contains the essence. The stated themes of the plays are the major decisions that Prospero makes: the forgiveness of his enemies and the renunciation of his magic. The 'colonial' interpretation, as far as it can be justified, lies in Prospero's relationship to Ariel and Caliban. Ariel keeps demanding his freedom, while Caliban claims the island has been taken from him, but the island and the characters are part of a fairy story. They may have a metaphorical life but the play is not about a society.

When I was an undergraduate I appeared in a production of the play by the Oxford don Nevill Coghill. It took place by the lake in Worcester College garden. I was one of the lords. At the end we sailed away with Prospero across the lake in a boat. Ariel ran on the water (on carefully concealed duckboards) blowing kisses to his departing master, while Caliban waved cheerfully from the bank. This was a grossly sentimental interpretation, which would be unthinkable now. In a more recent RSC production, Ariel spat at Prospero after he has been given his freedom. This is equally crass. Ariel, like Mr Spock in *Star Trek*, has no feeling, though like Spock he is aware of it in others ('Mine would, sir, were I human'). His only desire is for his freedom, whatever that may represent. Caliban too wants freedom to repossess the island but sensually not socially.

In our time opinion has swung against all authority figures, some of whom the Victorians would have seen as essentially benevolent. Lear, the Duke in *Measure for Measure*, and Prospero are all suspect nowadays and it is true that they are all more complex than the benevolent paternalists of some earlier productions ('The old fantastical duke of dark corners'). It's also true that Prospero enjoys exercising his magic power, that he wants to run everyone's lives, but that does not make him a colonial exploiter. The island is uninhabited by humans: Ariel is a spirit and Caliban is a monster. There are no natives to be exploited. Jonathan Miller, who was one of the first to promote the colonial interpretation, cast two very earthbound black actors as Caliban and Ariel to justify it. He had his natives but he had lost two of the meaningful symbols of the play—the being who is all air and the one who is all earth. They may represent many things—Ariel the superego and Caliban the id, for example—but they have to retain their identity in the fairy story for the interpretation to work. The moment you make them human the play becomes ordinary and unmagical. You can transfer the metaphor to another period and still keep the basic elements. This was wonderfully done in the film *Forbidden Planet*, loosely based on *The Tempest*. Ariel was a robot and Caliban was an unknown monster attacking the space station. (In the end the monster is revealed as the scientist's unconscious desires. We have symbol and meaning together.)

Miller is a rationalist and opposed to magic. He sees *Alice in Wonderland* as a critique of Victorian society—which in part it is, but it is still about a little girl who falls down a rabbit hole and meets strange creatures and live playing cards. It may be 'about' social repressions, but we have to experience that through the story and the fantastic nature of the characters. *The Magic Flute* may be a metaphor of the Age of Enlightenment, but if you set it in an eighteenth-century library, as Miller did, the magic disappears. All fairy stories strike at things deep in the unconscious, but the moment you bring their meaning to the surface or rationalise them in terms of society, they lose their power. Which may be all right for psychotherapy but it is death in the theatre.

Plays, even plays like *The Tempest*, are not just fairy stories. Characters exist in social relationships which are recognisable. Their conversations reveal philosophies which are part of the culture and the beliefs of their time. They make jokes about contemporary events that are incomprehensible to future generations—at least, they do in Shakespeare, whose plays are full of verbal material of all kinds that is capable of a political slant. But when seen on the stage today they must create their own world. It is up to an audience to make the connection with our world as it watches the play.

The Tempest is interesting structurally. It obeys the unities: the action takes place on the island in just one day. Shakespeare keeps reminding us of the passage of time. It's now or never for Prospero. The form of the play and its stated themes are unusually clear: the renunciation of magic and the forgiveness of enemies. They are embedded in the narrative structure. An idea like colonialism may be sparked by particular scenes or particular lines but does not grow organically. It is a concept brought from the outside which distorts the whole.

It's my job as a director to make sense of the structure of words and actions we call a play. Like any reader or member of an audience I have some sense of what its overall meaning is, what it all adds up to, and I try to be honest and not make it mean only what I would like it to mean. My lifeline and my discipline is the narrative, the story—not just the basic elements of the plot but also how much of the play each part of the action takes up. In the process of rehearsal I may get absorbed in the detail, noting the character of the language, the repetition of the imagery, but above all, I am involved in the actors' creative process and it is my job to keep their focus on what is happening in the scene and what is happening in the play. I may stress one side of the narrative to clarify or intensify the play's meaning, but this is not the same thing as imposing a concept.

One of the first productions in which I was aware of the interpretation of the play through the action, rather than as a clever visual presentation, was Tyrone Guthrie's *Henry VIII* (Stratford, 1949/50 and Old Vic, 1953). Guthrie was the first British director to establish himself as being as important a figure as the leading actor. *Henry VIII* is, for the most part, a pedestrian piece, which Shakespeare was dragged back from retirement to touch up, at least half of it the work of Fletcher. It suited the taste of the time with its opportunities for spectacle in the coronation procession and the dream of Queen Katherine, both described in great detail in the stage directions in a most un-Shakespearean way. It has fine things in it, though, particularly in the writing of the scenes for Katherine and Wolsey, and the casting of those parts with leading actors like Ellen Terry and Henry Irving was the usual justification for the revival of the play. This unbalances the play and loses what narrative structure there is. Guthrie took a different approach. He built the play round the King, which is a rather underwritten part, and, although he had good actors in all the parts, there was no indulgence of the death scenes of Katherine and Wolsey. There was a permanent set with an off-centre staircase, as was Guthrie's custom; the lighting throughout was bright, even in the night scenes when darkness was indicated by lit torches. This was my first experience of what was later called Brechtian lighting. The action hurtled across the stage, characters were literally swept out of the way by the movement of history and the ruthlessness of Henry. Buckingham, Wolsey and Katherine had to make way for the violent imperative of the Protestant Reformation. The first half ended with what in the original is usually a minor moment, in which Cranmer is summoned to be Henry's frontman. In Guthrie's production, on the King's line 'My learned and well-belovèd servant Cranmer', a little man crept out of a group of clerics, and Anthony Quayle as Henry put his arm round Cranmer's shoulder and started to whisper in his ear—words which we could not hear, never written by Shakespeare or Fletcher. Back and forth they walked as the house lights came up for the interval. The audience saw history in the making. The drive of the play was not individuals but political necessity. Interestingly, Guthrie avoided the obvious opportunities for spectacle in the coronation, which was described through the eyes of bystanders, or in Katherine's dream, which was seen through the eyes of the actress. The whole play became a build-up to the outrageous royal flattery of the last scene, when a glorious future is promised for the infant Elizabeth; bells sounded and banners were waved. This was made doubly significant by the identification of the baby with the approaching accession of our present Queen—indeed, by the time of the Old Vic production she was being crowned.

Guthrie had given a shapeless play what Stanislavsky called the 'through-line', the spine which would keep the whole play together. Did he distort the original? Well, perhaps, but it did not contradict the basic action of the play. (Terence Gray—an early, irreverent director of the 1930s—showed his contempt for the last scene by throwing the baby into the audience.) Guthrie made the play state more clearly what the authors wanted it to mean.

19
Words and Music

Strauss's opera *Capriccio* is based on a charming conceit. It concerns a countess who has two lovers, a poet and a composer, and cannot choose between them. It is a metaphor for opera itself. Which is more important, words or music? Strauss had worked with distinguished writers like Hugo von Hofmannsthal and knew how complex and difficult the relationship was between composer and poet. But in opera is there really any contest? Don't most people go to the opera for the music, or more precisely the music with the drama—and the more emotional the better? They don't go for the *words* and the music. In this country, at any rate, the words are usually in a foreign language, and even when they are in English you can't hear them. This is now admitted by the use of surtitles above the proscenium, a device invented for simultaneous translation of foreign opera, which is now used to tell us what the words are in our own language.

Words carry intellectual ideas, social commentary, complex imagery which cannot be expressed in music. Music enters our senses and stirs our emotions directly. You can listen to music without thinking. Words more easily explore irony and ambiguity, those staples of English poetry. The marriage of words and music is a risky business. Most of the best operas are based on second-rate plays like Dumas' *La Dame aux Camélias* (*La Traviata*), Sardou's melodrama *Tosca* or Belasco's *Madame Butterfly*. Verdi got away with *Otello* because Shakespeare's play is nearly an opera in the emotional melodrama of its plot, but even then the character of Iago is less complex, less interesting than the original. *Falstaff*, a great opera, is based on the most boring of all Shakespeare's plays. One huge exception has to be *The Marriage of Figaro*. Beaumarchais' play is a great comedy, but Mozart's opera is even greater. Da Ponte's libretto is a masterly editing of the text; the flow of the narrative never seems held up by the music. The arias are just the right length for their dramatic content and catch the very essence of the original. The moment at the end of Act 2 when eight characters express their reaction to the same situation at the same time is something that no dramatist can ever achieve.

Sometimes original works are made by writer and composer working together. Rodgers and Hart, Brecht and Weill in *The Threepenny Opera*, Strauss and Hofmannsthal. The taking of words which already exist to be spoken in a play, and setting them to music, whether in opera or musical, or the interspersing of songs into an original play, is more questionable. I can't swallow it when a tenor starts to sing 'I know a bank where the wild thyme blows', a beautiful speech when spoken, but cumbersome when sung. I want to cry out, 'It's not meant to be sung!' The play is perfect anyway and has enough music of its own. You could argue that *Pygmalion* and *My Fair Lady* are separate works, just as *West Side Story* is not *Romeo and Juliet*. It's true that very few of Shaw's actual words are set to music, and then usually odd phrases, but the Lerner and Loewe musical does include chunks of the original play between the numbers. There is always a jolt when the play's dialogue has to shift into the musical form, though in performance the fact that Rex Harrison spoke rather than sang his numbers concealed this. The pace at which the action of a play unfolds through the dialogue is an essential part of its nature.

This is even more true of a poem. When you first read this poem by Blake:

O Rose thou art sick!
The invisible worm
That flies in the night,
In the howling storm,
Has found out thy bed
Of crimson joy:
And his dark secret love
Does thy life destroy.

—you experience it as an action, something you live through without pause. Who will ever forget it? It is a living thing. When Britten sets it to music in his *Serenade* you get his commentary on the poem but not the original work. It may be beautiful, but it can never introduce you to the poem's meaning. The musical action doesn't carry you through the experience. All short poems have an action; a sonnet, for instance, has an unmistakable development with a conclusion. To set them to music always weakens their dynamic movement. There are some glorious exceptions: Schubert in *Erlkönig* carries us along in the narrative without a break, the accompaniment of the horse's hooves heightening the tension. In *Gretchen at the Spinning Wheel* he takes the scene from Goethe's *Faust* in which Gretchen expresses her feelings in a poem of the utmost simplicity with a refrain. Using the sound of the whirring wheel as the musical background, he takes us through the dilemma of the girl, her anguish mixed with pleasure, which climaxes in 'and O, his kiss'. It has a cyclic movement that never loses the drive of the original. Most Schubert songs are shaped as a single developing action. You start at the beginning, go through an emotional experience which is resolved, and then come to rest. They are miniature plays. Both the songs I cite use a repetitive rhythmic accompaniment to maintain the movement and the dramatic tension.

Shakespeare always knew how to use music in his plays sparingly, sometimes placing songs at key moments to create a shift of mood, and most significantly as part of the action: to work Prospero's magic in *The Tempest*, and to bring the statue to life in *The Winter's Tale*. Music is nearly always used in the later plays to signify resolution and reconciliation, the return to harmony and order. In *Twelfth Night* the three wonderful songs set the play's unusual melancholy character. If you add more music to these plays you lessen the impact of the music that is already there. The cinema has conditioned us to expect a usually continuous musical accompaniment to the most banal scenes. The word 'melodrama' originally meant drama with music. The music supplies the emotions that the writer cannot write or the actors cannot act—or, worse, overstates what is already there. Stephen Daldry's production of *An Inspector Calls* had music nearly all the way through it, a kind of muzak for the theatre.

Brecht was very clear about what he felt when he wrote:

> Mark off clearly the songs from the rest.
> Make it clear that this is where
> The sister art enters the play.
> Announce it by some emblem summoning music,
> By a shift of lighting
> By a caption
> By a picture.

—and in his production of *Mother Courage* an emblem of drums and flags was flown in at the beginning of each song and out at the end. During the play it became more and more ragged.

I know I am in a minority. Opera is the most admired form. The rich can wallow in a good night out and get their culture without pain. You can see them night after night at Covent Garden, together with the politicians, lapping up High Art in a Centre of Excellence. Shakespeare plus Verdi must be better than Shakespeare neat. Most people think music the greater art, and the more of it the better. Musicals dominate the West End theatre, and there has been a knock-on effect in the production of classic plays which are treated as a kind of poor man's musical, often directed by the same director who made his fortune directing musicals in the commercial theatre. It has led to a flattening out of the experience of what theatre can be.

20
State of Play

Looking back over what I have written I see that the only actors I cite as models were already established stars when I was still at school. As a boy I saw Gielgud in his last *Hamlet* on the stage, Olivier in the film of *Henry V*, and heard Evans as Rosalind on the radio. They set standards of delivery which I still respect. I think probably no actor today is accepted as a similar authority by a younger generation. This is not because the older actors were better but because they had the status of their experience.

A leading actor had his or her name above the title. On the posters there were two, three and even four sizes of billing to indicate the relative importance, and usually salary, of all the actors. A play without a name over the title was unthinkable. The right to star billing was related in some way to the actor's talent, experience and attractiveness to the public. When the Royal Court, the Royal Shakespeare Company and the National Theatre all began with a resident company it was agreed that actors should be listed alphabetically with equal billing. All three theatres subsequently gave up the idea of a permanent ensemble but equality of billing continued (though there are other ways of conveying who is playing the leading part). But on publicity material the director, the designer, the lighting designer—and now even the sound designer—have precedence over the actors. On television, the cast lists whizz past so quickly that you cannot read the names of the actors and the characters they played.

Even more humiliating, the list is now squeezed to the side, while some forthcoming programme is trailed. When you watch a rerun of television drama of an earlier decade, like *Tinker, Tailor, Soldier, Spy*, the credits roll majestically by with time to read the names of the actors and the parts they played. Indeed, the tempo of the editing, and the pace of the playing of the whole piece, is quite different from today. Guinness's performance is almost as slow as the Noh theatre and just as wonderful.

This is not just nostalgia for a vanished age. The devaluing of the actor has certainly affected the work. After the death of Irving in 1905, the advent of the cinema and later of televison meant that actors would work in more than one medium. Very few actors today have developed their craft only on the stage. Films and television do not require the same projection of voice or personality. The new media often demand a greater naturalism than expected in the theatre. (Interestingly, the theatre was becoming more naturalistic at the point the cinema was invented.) It is still possible to be known as a film star by your own name, but on the television you are more likely to be known by the name of the part you play. Many young actors do not aspire to play Hamlet or Hedda Gabler. They think themself lucky to be in *EastEnders*.

Most of the essays in this book are concerned with how the written word is brought to life on the stage. The use of language requires sensitivity not only in the actor's craft but in the ear of the audience, and the former is worthless without the latter. Plays are still performed on stages for the most part, without amplification (but for how much longer?). A long speech or a long sentence requires the same control of delivery as when there was no cinema or television. The tunes the actor's voice makes may use fewer variations of pitch to be acceptable to the modern ear, but the writing must have the same shape and flow and dynamic in relation to the text that they always had. And it's not only speaking a classic text but also exploring the range and discipline of a contemporary play through the voice. Many actors no longer live through the voice as a prime means of expression. It is not a question of speaking beautifully or of speaking 'RP' (Irving was considered to have an ugly voice with idiosyncratic vowels), but of being capable of communicating as much through speech as through the body.

Do we have to be content to admit that dramatic writing can never have the power it did? An audience's vocabulary is shrinking all the time and the need for visual stimulus grows daily. But the range of new plays to be seen is greater than ever. We have a National Theatre whose repertoire is made up of more than fifty per cent new and contemporary work, unlike the state theatres of any other country. This must be in large measure due to the stimulus to new writing given by George Devine at the Royal Court Theatre more than fifty years ago. Now it is unusual for a play by a young writer of talent not to find a home. Writing has changed and developed with the changes in the spoken language, and makes new demands on the actor. No good writer thinks of his or her play as literature to be preserved for the stages of future generations but is writing to express something he or she wants to say now. In fact, I would suggest that writers today are less concerned with literary quality than their fellow novelists are. Not enough of them write only for the theatre and their plays would be equally at home on television. But theatre language must have its own life, the best words and actions, if it is to survive. Writers must fight the tendency to think that speaking is just a continuation of everyday conversation rather than something over which they have charge. The first scene of *Hamlet* may sound like people talking in colloquial language, but Claudius at prayer certainly does not. Writing may no longer be in verse but it can still be poetic if we accept that the sequence of the actions may be as much part of the poetry of theatre as the language.

Actors still have great awareness of language and its use in the theatre by writers of their own time. After Harold Pinter died there was a celebration of his work in a performance at the National Theatre. A group of some twenty actors sat in a great arc across the width of the Olivier stage and got up to play scenes from Pinter's plays, most of which had been memorised, but with minimal staging. Many of the actors had played the parts in productions but they all brought a love of the writer's work and a responsibility to its performance on the stage that one rarely sees. This was a celebration of a writer's language with no intellectual concept to get in the way. It was a demonstration of what Beckett meant when he said that a theatre stage is an area of maximum verbal presence and maximum corporeal presence. In a writer of their own time the actors had all the authority of Gielgud or Olivier or Evans. Whether they could display the same authority in a classical text is another matter, but it was heartening to see theatre in which words had so much value and yet the actors were so physically alive.

There is a tendency to speak of 'text-based work' as if it were a small and decaying part of theatre. All plays are 'text-based' and whatever the changes in language, they always will be. You cannot have a theatre without words and ideas. 'Physical theatre' should not mean mindless theatre. Audiences will always find it easier to watch spectacle than think, but would feel starved if deprived of ideas indefinitely. Much recent work has absorbed mime, music and technology into a mixed-media experience, sometimes very imaginatively and successfully, but a theatre needs plays. A play is still a structure in which characters move through a series of actions, speaking words to each other to make a meaningful experience.

We cannot return to Shakespeare's collective when writer and actors were equal shareholders in the theatre venture and did not include a director. We cannot live forever in the shadow of Beckett and Brecht. Theatre workers need their freedom. We have to find the writer/actor/director balance for our own time. Certainly my best work at the Royal Court, the National Theatre and most of all with the Joint Stock Theatre Group was when the work came nearest to that of a collective. Today the amount of talent in writing and acting is enormous, but not enough is focused or shared. We live in an individualistic, competitive society, but does it have to dominate our work?

Index

Alchemist, The   103–4, 108
Alexander, F.M.   59
Alfreds, Mike   55
Alice in Wonderland   147
All That Fall   45–7
Allio, René   xi
Almeida Theatre (London)
   15–16
Anderson, Lindsay   3–4, 7, 52
Antony and Cleopatra   72, 124,
   135–6
Arden, John   1, 10, 100
Aristotle   15, 17, 134
Arts Theatre (London)   10
As You Like It   157
Ashcroft, Peggy   72, 142
Ayckbourn, Alan   53

Baal   10, 52
Bagnold, Enid   74
Barber of Seville, The   140
Barrault, Jean-Louis   72
Barter, Noriko   66
Bartholomew Fair   108
Barton, John   136
Bateson, F.W.   77–8
Beaumarchais, Pierre-Augustin
   152
Beaux' Stratagem, The   xi
Beckett, Samuel   x, 4, 10–13, 17,
   24, 29–30, 42–7, 52, 67–8, 72,
   93–8, 103, 160–1

Belasco, David   151
Bells, The   58
Benny, Jack   28
Berger, John   7, 9, 12
Berliner Ensemble   x, 7–10, 13,
   43–4, 51, 72–3
Bernstein, Leonard   152
Blackfriars Theatre (1609)   13,
   41
Blair, Tony   81
Blake, William   128, 152–3
Blakely, Colin   xi
Blin, Roger   42
Bond, Edward   xi, 3–4, 45,
   49–51, 77
Bourgeois gentilhomme, Le   115
Brando, Marlon   67
Brecht, Bertolt   x, 7–10,
   12–13, 17, 37, 43–4, 50–2,
   63, 72–4, 100, 103, 149, 152,
   154, 161
Bremner, Rory   102
Bridie, James   144
Britten, Benjamin   153
Brook, Peter   44, 99
Bunyan, John   123–5
Busch, Ernst   10

Calder-Marshall, Anna   xi
Callas, Maria   140–1
Candida   125
Capriccio   151

Carroll, Lewis (Charles Dodgson) 133, 147
Carver, Raymond 39–40
Cathedral 39–40
Caucasian Chalk Circle, The 7–8, 63, 100
Central School of Speech and Drama 142
Chalk Garden, The 74
Changing Room, The 52
Chaplin, Charlie 101
Chekhov, Anton xi, 16–19, 38, 42, 51, 95–6
Cherry Orchard, The 17, 19
Churchill, Caryl 45, 48–9
Churchill, Winston 80–2
Citizen Kane 101
Cocktail Party, The 116
Coghill, Nevill 146
Coleridge, S.T. 5, 61
Comédie-Française 72
Commedia dell'Arte 3, 99, 100
Congreve, William 74, 89–92, 144
Copeau, Jacques 3, 99
Coriolanus 65, 95
Coward, Noël 38, 47, 86, 93, 125
Cromwell, Oliver 125
Cymbeline 41

Daldry, Stephen 154
Dame aux camélias, La 151
Dante Alighieri 11
Da Ponte, Lorenzo 152
Daphne Laureola 144
Decroux, Étienne 72
Delaney, Shelagh 4
Devine, George 1–4, 10–12, 51, 99, 159
Dexter, John 3, 52
Dickens, Charles 88–9, 101, 108

D'Oyly Carte Opera 44–5
Drunk Enough to Say I Love You? 49
Duchess of Malfi, The 78–9
Duck Soup 38
Dumas, Alexandre, *fils* 151
Duse, Eleonora 58

Early Morning 77
East 15 (*see* Theatre Royal, Stratford East)
Eliot, T.S. 115–16
Endgame 10–11, 44, 98
English Stage Company 1–5
Entertainer, The 10, 101
Erlkönig, Der 153
Essay on Man, An 58
Etherege, George 38, 125
Evans, Edith xi, 74, 90, 142–4, 157, 160
Exposed by the Mask 36, 117

Falstaff 152
Fanshen 63
Farquhar, George xi
Faust 153
Fergusson, Francis 19
Fin de partie 10–11 (and see *Endgame*)
Fletcher, John 149–50
Fogerty, Elsie 142
Folio and Quarto texts (Shakespeare) 29–30, 88, 116
Footfalls 43, 46, 97
Forbidden Planet 147
4.48 Psychosis 49
Fraser, Neal 46–7
Freud, Sigmund 63–4

Garrick, David 58
Geneva 125
George Dandin 72

Giacometti, Alberto   72
Gielgud, John   xi, 65, 67, 74,
   142, 144, 157, 160
Gilbert and Sullivan   44–5
Gill, Peter   3, 18, 45, 48, 92
Globe Theatre (1599)   13, 35, 41
Goethe, Johann Wolfgang von
   153
Granville Barker, Harley   42
Gray, Terence   150
Gretchen at the Spinning Wheel
   153
Guide to English Literature, A
   77–8
Guinness, Alec   xi, 101, 158
Gunter, John   xi
Guthrie, Tyrone   64, 71, 149–50

Hall, Peter   10–11, 36, 84, 99,
   117
Hamlet   16, 19, 21–33, 36–7, 39,
   41, 56, 58, 61, 64, 66, 79–80,
   84, 88, 109–11, 115–21, 124,
   127, 135–9, 142, 157–9
Hamlet (1948 film)   28, 64
Hampton, Christopher   ix–xii
Handel, George Frideric   91
Happy Days   11, 42–3, 44
Happy Haven, The   100
Hare, David   3, 63
Harris, Rosemary   11–12
Harrison, Rex   152
Hedda Gabler   66, 158
Henry IV, Parts 1 and 2   112–13,
   116–17
Henry V   23, 35–6, 82, 135, 138,
   142, 157
Henry V (1945 film)   35–7, 138,
   142, 157
Henry VI, Part 3   65–6
Henry VIII   149–50
'Her Triumph' ('A Celebration of
   Charis')   104–5

Herbert, Jocelyn   3, 10, 51–2
Hofmannsthal, Hugo von
   151–2
Hugo, Victor   72
Hunter, Kathryn   44
Hurwicz, Angelika   7–8

Ibsen, Henrik   15–19, 31, 66,
   158
Idea of a Theater, The   19
Importance of Being Earnest, The
   74, 75–6, 91–2, 143
Inspector Calls, An   154
Ionesco, Eugène   11
Irving, Henry   57–8, 74, 149,
   158

Jellicoe, Ann   1
Jew of Malta, The   78, 108
John Gabriel Borkman   17
Johnson, Samuel   62
Joint Stock Theatre Group   39,
   63, 101, 161
Jones, Ernest   64
Jonson, Ben   91, 103–5, 108,
   125
Joyce, James   92–3
Julius Caesar   24–5, 67, 75, 82, 90,
   131
Julius Caesar (1953 film)   67

Kane, Sarah   49
Kermode, Frank   130
Kidd, Robert   x
King Lear   16, 32, 65, 109, 124,
   146–7
Kinuta (The Fulling Block)   69–71
Kitchen, The   52
Krapp's Last Tape   11

Laban, Rudolf   59
Laughton, Charles   43–4
Lawrence, D.H.   18

Lean, David 101
Lerner and Loewe 152
Life of Galileo, The 37, 43–4
Little Eyolf 16
Littlewood, Joan 4–5, 37
Logue, Christopher 7
Look Back in Anger 1, 3
Losey, Joseph 43–4
Love's Labour's Lost 107–8, 117
Lubitsch, Ernst 28
Lynn, Ralph 97

Macbeth 13, 16, 38–9, 41, 62–3, 112, 120, 124, 127–31
Macbeth (opera) 140–1
Macdonald, James 49
MacGowran, Jack 11
Madame Butterfly 151
Madras House, The 42
Magic Flute, The 147
Malade imaginaire, Le 42
Malleson, Miles 109
Man of Mode, The 38
Marceau, Marcel 72
Marlowe, Christopher 78, 108, 112
Marriage of Figaro, The 152
Marvell, Andrew 125
Marx, Groucho 38
Master Builder, The 17
Measure for Measure 146–7
Merchant of Venice, The 101, 108
Merry Wives of Windsor, The 152
Michelangelo 99
Middleton, Thomas 21
Midsummer Night's Dream, A 117
Miller, Jonathan 147
Mills, John 139–40
Milton, John 82, 91, 125
Misanthrope, Le 71–2
Molière 42, 71–2, 115
Monty Python's Flying Circus 2

Mother Courage 8, 17, 37, 43–4, 72–3, 154
Moscow Art Theatre 42, 95–6
Mozart, Wolfgang Amadeus 103, 147, 152
Much Ado About Nothing 115, 117
My Fair Lady 152

National Theatre (London) 11, 157, 159–61
Neher, Caspar 10
Nemirovich-Danchenko, Vladimir 42
No Man's Land 76–7
Not I 42–3, 67–8
Number, A 45, 48–9

Odd Man Out 47
Oedipus Rex 19, 31, 101
Old Hat, The 9
Old Times 45, 47
Old Vic Theatre (London) 43, 149–50
Oliver Twist (1948 film) 101
Olivier, Laurence xi, 12, 23, 28, 35–7, 46, 64–6, 101, 138, 139, 142, 160
O'Neill, Eugene 38
Optimistic Thrust, An 101
Orwell, George 111
Osborne, John 1, 3, 10, 101
Otello 51–2
Othello 35, 61–2, 64–5, 113, 124, 151–2
Otway, Thomas 125–6

Page, Anthony xi, 15–16
Palace Theatre (London) 7–10
Paradise Lost 82
Pennington, Michael 28
Phèdre 72
Phillips, Andy 52

Philoctetes 11–12
Pickwick Papers, The 88–9
Pinter, Harold 38, 45, 47, 50, 76–7, 86, 97, 160
Piscator, Erwin 44
Play 11–12, 17, 42–3, 93–4, 98
Plowright, Joan 46
Plummer, Christopher 143–4
Poel, William 142
Pope, Alexander 58
Priestley, J.B. 154
Private Lives 47
Proust, Marcel 86
Puccini, Giacomo 151
Pygmalion 152

Quayle, Anthony 149–50

Racine, Jean 72
Rape of Lucrece, The 116
Redgrave, Michael 72
Renaud, Madeleine 72
Resounding Tinkle, A 2, 94–5
Revenger's Tragedy, The 21
Richard II 82–3
Richard III 23, 35, 64–6, 136–7, 143–4
Richardson, Ralph 64, 101
Richardson, Tony 3
Rimbaud, Arthur x
Robeson, Paul 65
Rockaby 44
Rodgers and Hart 152
Romeo and Juliet 41, 74, 95, 109, 152
Rosmersholm 15–18, 31
Rossini, Gioachino 140
Royal Academy of Dramatic Art (RADA) 13, 29–33, 38–9, 45–7, 69, 99, 142
Royal Court Theatre ix–xi, 1–5, 7, 10–11, 13, 50–2, 100, 157, 159, 161

Royal Opera House, Covent Garden 154
Royal Shakespeare Company (RSC) 63, 72, 100, 146, 157
Royal Shakespeare Theatre (Stratford) 28, 41, 143–4, 149–50

Saint Joan of the Stockyards 10
Saint-Denis, Michel 3, 99
Sardou, Victorien 151
Saved 45, 49–51
Scarlet Pimpernel, The 144
Schubert, Franz 153
Schut, Henk 32–3, 69
Scofield, Paul xi
Seagull, The 16–17, 38
Sedgwick, Toby 46–7
Serenade 153
Shakespeare, William xiii, 13, 22–4, 35, 37, 39, 41, 56–7, 62–3, 65, 84, 91, 97, 103–5, 107–13, 115–21, 123–5, 135, 139, 142, 148, 153–4, 160–1 (*and see under individual plays*)
Shakespeare's Sonnets 104–5, 116–17
Shaw, George Bernard 86, 96, 123–5, 152
'Sick Rose, The' 152–3
Simpson, N.F. 2–3, 10, 94–5
Small Change 45, 48
Smith, Maggie xi, 90–1, 144
Sophocles 11–12, 18–19, 31, 101
Speakers, The 39
Stafford-Clark, Max 15, 39, 55
Stanislavsky, Konstantin 42, 55–6, 59, 63–4, 73–4, 101, 102, 150
Stephens, Robert 11–12
Sterne, Laurence 2
Storey, David 3–4, 10, 52

Strange Interlude 38
Strauss, Richard 151–2
Streetcar Named Desire, A 37–8
Suzuki, Tadashi 59

Tamburlaine the Great 112
Taste of Honey, A 4
Tempest, The 101, 105, 108–9, 145–8, 154
Terry, Ellen 74, 149
Terry, Fred 144
Théâtre Marigny (Paris) 72
Théâtre Nationale Populaire (Paris) 72–3
Theatre Royal, Stratford East (London) 4–5
Theatre Workshop 4–5
Three Sisters 42
Threepenny Opera, The 9, 152
Thurburn, Gwynneth 142
Tinker, Tailor, Soldier, Spy 158
To Be or Not To Be 28
Tosca 151
Total Eclipse x
Tourneur, Cyril 21
Traviata, La 151
Troilus and Cressida 16
Twelfth Night 57, 108, 110, 123, 139, 154
Tynan, Kenneth 2, 7, 11–12, 58

Ulysses 92–3
Uncle Vanya xi

Venice Preserv'd 125–6
Venus and Adonis 116

Verdi, Giuseppe 140–1, 151–2, 154
Verlaine, Paul x
Vilar, Jean 72–3
Voice of Poetry, The 142
Voysey Inheritance, The 42

Waiting for Godot 2, 10–12, 17, 24, 29–30, 42–4, 72, 93–7
Walton, William 142
Way of the World, The 74, 89–92, 144
Webster, John 78–9
Weigel, Helene 8–10, 52
Weill, Kurt 152
Welles, Orson 101
Wesker, Arnold 1, 3, 10, 52
Wesker Trilogy, The 10, 52
West Side Story 152
When We Dead Awaken 16
Whitelaw, Billie 11–12
Widowing of Mrs Holroyd, The 18
Wilde, Oscar 74, 75–6, 86, 91–2, 143
Williams, Heathcote 39
Williams, Tennessee 37–8
Williamson, Nicol 84
Wilson, Robert 73–4
Winter's Tale, The 85, 154

York Realist, The 48

Zeami 69–71, 73
Zeffirelli, Franco 28